P9-DNA-878

Comprehension
Connections

Bridges to
Strategic
Reading

Tanny McGregor

HEINEMANN
Portsmouth, NH

Heinemann

361 Hanover Street
Portsmouth, NH 03801–3912
www.heinemann.com

Offices and agents throughout the world

© 2007 by Tanny McGregor

All rights reserved. No part of this book may be reproduced in any form or by any electronic or mechanical means, including information storage and retrieval systems, without permission in writing from the publisher, except by a reviewer, who may quote brief passages in a review.

Library of Congress Cataloging-in-Publication Data
McGregor, Tanny.
   Comprehension connections : bridges to strategic reading / Tanny McGregor.
     p. cm.
   Includes bibliographical references and index.
   ISBN-13: 978-0-325-00887-5 (alk. paper)
   ISBN-10: 0-325-00887-6
1. Reading comprehension.   2. Reading, Psychology of.   3. Metacognition in children.   I. Title.
   LB1050.45.M34 2007
   372.62'3—dc22
                                            2006034856

Editor: Harvey Daniels
Production editor: Sonja S. Chapman
Cover and interior designs: Gina Poirier
Cover photographs: Miles McGregor
Interior photographs: Miles and Tanny McGregor
Compositor: Gina Poirier
Manufacturing: Steve Bernier

Printed in the United States of America on acid-free paper
17 16 15 14   VP   12 13 14 15

To Miles

Contents

Foreword

Imagine learning to dance when the dancers around you are all invisible. Imagine learning a sport when the players who already know the game can't be seen. Bizarre as this may sound, something close to it happens all the time in one very important area of learning: learning to think. Thinking is pretty much invisible. To be sure, sometimes people explain the thoughts behind a particular conclusion, but often they do not. Mostly thinking happens under the hood, with the marvelous engine of our mindbrain." —*David Perkins 2003*

Harvard professor David Perkins is right. Thinking does not reveal itself fully dressed on a platter. It lurks offstage, behind the curtain. It is the job of every teacher to raise the curtain and make our thinking visible and concrete for the eager audience that waits each day. Much of the recent work in reading comprehension instruction has focused on making thinking visible. In that vein, we model a repertoire of strategies that support readers to understand what they read. Using schema, asking questions, inferring, visualizing, determining importance and synthesizing information will make a difference in the reading lives of our kids. However, these thinking strategies are abstract and understanding how a strategy leads to comprehension can be tough to fathom.

Enter *Comprehension Connections*, the book you hold in your hands. Tanny McGregor's book brims with ideas, lessons and projects that make abstract thinking visible and concrete for our kids, so they can *understand their thinking and think to understand*. The strategies described in this book are not merely reading strategies; they are thinking strategies. We make connections, ask questions and infer every single day whether we pick up a piece of text or not. We determine what is most important to remember and synthesize information at every turn in our lives. We think when we listen, we think when we view, and we think when we read. If we teach thinking strategies outside of text before teaching them within, our kids just may have a more seamless transition as they use and apply strategies flexibly in their reading.

Comprehension Connections is filled to bursting with ideas to engage kids and nudge them to think. I love the famous thinker quotes that pepper the chapters, such a great way to make kids aware of people who have made a difference, how they think and why it matters. I also greatly appreciate Tanny's use of art and music to prompt thinking throughout the book. In these days of dwindling resources for the arts where too many districts have narrowed the curriculum to simply teach what is tested, the importance of art and music cannot be overstated.

Thanks to Tanny, I was lucky to spend a morning watching a group of fourth graders as they engaged in a spirited and empathetic conversation about bullying after listening to the poignant song, *Rachel Delevoryas*. Before reading this book, I had never thought to use a Norman Rockwell painting or a Vermeer in a comprehension lesson. And how can you not love teaching kids to infer by going through a wastebasket and drawing conclusions about the family who owns it? This book is creative; but perhaps even more importantly, this book is *fun* for kids, teachers and readers.

So join Tanny as she works her magic in a variety of elementary classrooms at every grade level. Watch as she "jumpstarts" kids into the realm of thinking. Notice how she launches a strategy with a concrete experience before teaching the strategy in reading so her kids have an anchor to connect the new to the known. See how she infuses art, music, and movement into the daily routine. Don't miss how she builds in time every day for independent reading where kids read in texts of their choice and at their level to get plenty of practice thinking to enhance understanding. Tanny is a terrific educator with a lot to say. Her respect for and love of kids shines through on every page. Happy reading!

—Stephanie Harvey
November 2006

Perkins, David. 2003. "Making Thinking Visible" *New Horizons for Learning Online Journal* http://www.newhorizons.org/strategies/ thinking/perkins.htm December 2003.

Acknowledgments

the WC department of teaching & learning: angie ♥ karen ♥ lesley ♥ marcia ♥ matt ♥ m.e. wendy

miles 744

editors extraordinaire: ♥ lois bridges ♥ smokey daniels

the talented * teachers of the west * clermont schools

the 4 b's: bailey * bergen * blythe * brynne

mini~cooper ♥ mentors: steph harvey ~and~ debbie miller~

with ♥ from tanny

lime tic~tacs and diet peach snapple

candy: the girl next door

kj

Sherwood Schwartz, creator of the brady bunch

my ♥ kindergarten teacher... mrs. hendel

the littlest singers at CHPC

the sunshine state support system: dad & mom ~ janet ~ holly & austin

the lab rats~ becky ♥ mary ~ mike ♥ sally ~ sharon ♥ vera

graycie catalina

Prologue
Concrete Bridges:
The New Deal for Readers

r. Hagaman would be surprised! As a high school student in his American History class, I'm sure I gave Mr. H the impression that I wasn't paying attention. Strangely enough, I'm still thinking about Franklin Delano Roosevelt and the WPA! What FDR accomplished with the Works Progress Administration mirrors what I want to do with instruction. Has it been a while since you thought about the Roosevelt era? Let me refresh your memory.

Crisis plagued President Franklin Delano Roosevelt in 1933. The Great Depression had demolished lives, leaving Americans disillusioned and unemployed. In a courageous revival attempt, FDR proposed a series of bills that provided the basis for the New Deal. Congress supported the president in employing everyone from the common laborer to the highly educated. Of the many employment projects that emerged from the New Deal, one is most intriguing: the Works Progress Administration. The WPA was a massive employment program through which the jobless could work to construct, among other things, concrete bridges.

Thousands of Americans were empowered through the construction of these bridges, and many of these amazing structures still stand today. In essence, these concrete bridges were a link to the future. Jobs provided by the New Deal jump-started families out of the Great Depression and into their first semblance of financial security. I guess you could say that hope existed for many Americans in a very *concrete* way.

This is just what I want to do for children: provide concrete instruction that jump-starts them into the realm of strategic thinking. With each lesson I construct, I want to empower students with tools of language, building their confidence as they bridge the known to the new. For many of them it *will* be a new deal, where *thinking* replaces the *right answer*, where meaning is created and not simply received.

Other parallels exist between the Roosevelt era and the current state of teaching. Like today's teacher, FDR was in a fix! He felt solely responsible for the success of those who looked to him as their leader, even though he had limited time and resources. He faced criticism around every corner. Teachers can relate! "Never before have we had so little time in which to do so much." These words from FDR (Feb. 23, 1942 Fireside Chat) echo through schools across the country. Roosevelt had a tiny window of time to get people *working*; we have a tiny window of time to get kids *thinking*.

In my work as a literacy specialist, I collaborate with dozens of teachers each week, entry year and veteran alike. We teach and plan together, think and talk together. I have worked in the same suburban Cincinnati school district for many years, long enough to have developed deep, professional relationships with teachers in twelve schools. It's a great thing. We spend hours

Figure P–1 *WPA concrete bridge, Eden Park, Cincinnati, Ohio*

in each other's classrooms, seeking the heart of teaching and learning, striving to replace the superficial stuff. We're even getting pretty good at asking the hard questions and admitting when things are just not working. Take the afternoon when fifth-grade teacher Donna King tapped my shoulder and pulled me over to the side of the crowded hallway during class change. "OK, Tanny. You've got to help me. Where do I *start* when teaching comprehension strategies? It's all so abstract to the kids. I always thought that kids learn best when it's concrete for them, at least at first. It's true in math and science, anyway." I didn't have a concise, thoughtful answer for Donna that day, but I started wondering—a two-year quest, as a matter of fact. I thought about myself as a learner and yes, I do need concrete examples when trying to grasp something new. I recalled countless concrete experiences that I had afforded my students over the past eighteen years. I knew these experiences anchored their thinking, but I had never stopped to think about *why*. So thank you, Donna. Your questions have helped me clarify and develop my thinking about the launching of strategic instruction. Here's to you, Mr. Hagaman, and FDR!

Bridge Building 101

 purple onion, a shoehorn, a speckled rock. It has always seemed natural to use concrete items in my teaching; the students respond to them with enthusiasm and knowing smiles. Background knowledge is ready to tap, with most, if not all, students having connections to the objects. Perhaps it was through necessity that it started this way, since in my early years of teaching I had quite a tiny repertoire of instructional strategies! I would scrounge around for anything to make thinking come alive for my students. Or maybe I started using concrete items to launch lessons because I had listened to so many "object lessons" from my Grandpa Spaw, from Sunday school teachers, and camp counselors. These object lessons seemed to impact me in a deeper way than some other kinds of instruction; I would remember and ponder their meanings long after the lessons were through. Like the time my grandpa used the Spaw rosebush to teach my cousins and me about respect. Or the time my Brownie leader showed my troop how a funnel works in a lesson about making good choices. Through the concrete, the abstract became real, a kind of metaphorical miracle in my young mind. These lessons really got me *thinking*, and they seemed so fun! No text was involved, no writing, no worksheets...just lots of talk with people I cared about. Many of my teachers outside the school building were not formally educated, but they used this simple approach to cause me to think in profound ways. Author Kelly Gallagher refers to this in terms of "tangible" and "intangible" items. Gallagher writes,

"Repeated practice recognizing and analyzing metaphor enables students to generate their own metaphorical connections to the text and to the world, thus sharpening their higher-level thinking skills" (2004, 125). Little did I know that I would carry this age-old approach into my teaching career and merge it with contemporary research. Now I'm using concrete objects to craft "launching lessons": lessons that unleash new paths of thinking, lessons that support lots of student-to-student talk, lessons that can be referred to again and again, lessons that kids will remember and think about long after the school day is through.

Reading Is Thinking: Who Knew?

Remember all the hype around the coming millennium, aka Y2K? For many people, the year 2000 came and went without distinction. No power outages, computer crashes, or banking catastrophes. My thinking about reading instruction, however, was forever changed: I was introduced to the proficient reader research, synthesized by Pearson, Roehler, Dole, and Duffy (1992). Their work was just what the doctor ordered, a way to make sense of the increasingly complicated field of literacy. Pearson et al. isolated the thinking strategies that proficient readers consistently employ, straining the fact from the fluff. In other words, they simplified the dense mass of comprehension research, paring it down into a manageable chunk that teachers could digest and actually *use* to support kids. Imagine that!

I began to explore the strategies that amalgamate reading and thinking:

- **Using schema:** Thoughtful readers make connections, and retrieve and activate prior knowledge.

- **Inferring:** Thoughtful readers draw conclusions, make predictions, and form interpretations.

- **Questioning:** Thoughtful readers generate questions before, during, and after reading.

- **Determining importance:** Thoughtful readers sift out relevant and useful information.

■ **Visualizing:** Thoughtful readers create mental images supported by the five senses.

■ **Synthesizing:** Thoughtful readers continually change their thinking in response to text.

Investigating these strategies created fresh thinking for me, as it did for many of my teacher friends. We found ourselves meeting to talk about instruction in every spare moment: in school hallways, on the telephone, and at Starbucks. Over the next few years we immersed ourselves in professional reading, with a specific interest in comprehension. My colleagues and I became aware of our own reading processes, growing more metacognitive, intentionally sauntering through text instead of sprinting to the end. Many of us, myself included, who had spent much of the 1990s feeling bored and burned-out, were now finding joy and satisfaction in the work once again. We were more reflective than we had ever been. Creating lessons, developing book lists, and designing rubrics held new significance. Our enthusiasm spread throughout our schools, up and down the hallways. Many teachers plunged right in, ready for replacement practices in literacy. Others were more reticent, however, understanding the research but unsure of how to apply it. We all agreed on one thing, though. Sometimes the difficulty is in getting started, in trying to make the abstract real for our students and ourselves. Concrete.

Beginnings Matter

First impressions are critical to a learner. When introduced to a new thinking strategy, the learner instinctively asks, "Is this interesting? Do I need or want to know this? Can I succeed in thinking this way?" A concrete launching lesson helps students reply with a resounding yes to each of these questions. My friend Trisha teaches high school math. She sees her students shut down within seconds of attempting a new thinking process if she doesn't introduce it in a concrete way, if the language is too unfamiliar, if connections to existing knowledge aren't apparent, or if success isn't instantaneous. I know exactly what Trisha is talking about! In thinking about my instruction, I know there are times when I lose sight of the power of a solid beginning. This happens to me when I am feeling pressured to cover material instead of uncover thinking, when time is my rival. It's no accident that the lessons where I skimp on the beginning are the same lessons where the kids don't perform well at the end. Many of my colleagues agree; it happens to the best of us. We introduce a new strategy and a new text at the same time, expecting kids to decode and think metacognitively in a simultaneous fashion. We start with the abstract; no time for anything concrete. We plow through the modeling at breakneck speed. We don't capture time for think-alouds and guided discussion. With the clock as our enemy, we push forward, thinking more about the end result than the essential solid beginning. We need to change our minds. Sustained, meaningful beginnings are not a waste of our precious instructional time. It's quite the opposite! The pay-in now yields tremendous dividends later. We've got to remember that it's never a waste of time to teach kids to think. It bears repeating: beginnings matter.

The Beginning of the Beginning

One significant difference exists between the object lessons of my childhood and these concrete launching lessons I use with my students. The object lessons of my past were isolated, one-shot deals designed to get a point across. The concrete launches I use now are a jumping-off point, the spot where new thinking *begins*, the earliest place on the gradual-release-of-responsibility continuum, or GRR (Pearson and Gallagher 1983). Launching lessons, like buttermilk biscuits, are better when you start from scratch. My goal is still to guide my students toward independence, but I begin right where the kids *are*, not where I wish they were or where somebody else says they should be. In introducing a new strategy this way, I am zooming in on the first two components of the GRR continuum: teacher modeling and guided practice. I am firmly supporting students as they link what they already know to the kinds of thinking proficient readers employ.

The Launching Sequence

I didn't set out to create a formulaic path to follow for the launching of a strategy, but upon reflection, I discovered some instructional patterns had emerged. (See Figure 1–1.)

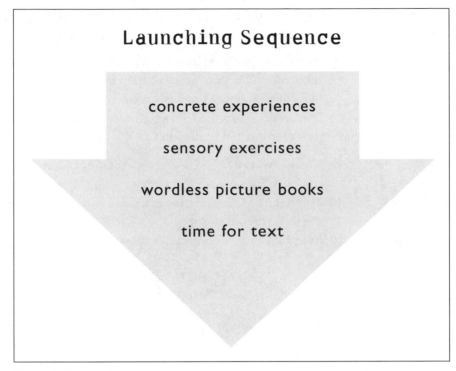

Figure 1–1 *Launching sequence*

This launching sequence was born from trial and error and a lot of talk with teachers. Allow me to define terms and explain each step in the launching sequence.

Note: This sequence consists of several lessons that span just a few days.

- **Launching sequence:** A progression for planning lessons that honors the gradual release of responsibility. This sequence allows time for teacher modeling, thinking aloud, and lots of talk. Kids acquire and practice strategic language, having fun along the way!

- **Concrete experience:** An initial exposure to a thinking strategy; a lesson with a concrete focus. Connections are easily made, creating bridges of thinking from the known to the new. Concrete lessons anchor future learning.

- **Sensory exercise:** A lesson that links the concrete experience with the ways kids learn, providing opportunities for practice in students' areas of strength, increasing their likelihood for success. Sensory exercises might include art, music, food, or movement.

■ **Wordless picture books:** Books with little or no text that enable the reader to practice strategic thinking without the added responsibility of decoding. Mistakenly considered by some to be baby books, wordless books provide a rich, authentic place for readers of all ages to rehearse strategic thinking.

■ **Time for text:** When the launching process is complete, learners confidently enter the world of text with strategic language in place. Through the launching sequence, kids acquire new tools for thinking; now they need time to practice using them. It's time for more independence, as support from the teacher decreases.

While working through the launching sequence, I've noticed a couple of things about my students. First of all, they appreciate the social context in which the strategies are introduced. In other words, they *love* the talk! I believe they *need* it, too. Reading is a social act. To promote deep thinking in our classrooms, we must build in time for talk. Kids crave interaction, and they will get it one way or another! We might as well capitalize on this inclination and provide opportunities for purposeful talk. *Turn and talk* is one way I assimilate more conversation into my instruction; it shows up in every launching sequence. When students are simply encouraged to turn and talk, *every student* gets the chance to be heard or to listen to a classmate, as compared with a more traditional approach where only one student is called upon at a time. I have observed authors Debbie Miller and Stephanie Harvey use turn and talk with great success; Debbie calls it "eye-to-eye and knee-to-knee," while Steph simply asks students to "turn to each other and talk." No matter what you call it, time for purposeful talk must be a priority.

Thinking stems are provided for each strategy, supporting kids as they begin to talk about their thinking. You'll see lists of these stems throughout this book. These lists have been compiled over the years, both through my professional reading and through listening to my students as they talked to each other. I model these stems in my teacher-student talk, and before too long I hear it in their student-to-student talk. I don't worry that kids are just parroting back the language; instead I celebrate that they are taking the language for a test drive. With continued opportunities for practice, they will soon be able to make it their own.

Although I don't promote placing labels on kids, I have noticed how certain kinds of learners respond to concrete experiences. Less-developed readers and thinkers are more than ready to experience something concrete in their otherwise abstract days at school; these kids appreciate concrete lessons in a profound way. They feel great about themselves because they get it right along with all of the other kids! Interestingly, highly developed readers and thinkers react in much the same way. Concrete experiences motivate these students to take their thinking to new heights. Having worked with gifted and talented students over the past few years, I know that these kids yearn to make a metaphor out of every new concept. Concrete experiences fulfill this need, providing an ideal opportunity for symbolic thinking through the creation of metaphor.

Another thing I've noticed is that more kids are willing to take risks as they participate in concrete lessons. Since kids have connections to concrete objects, every student knows a little something that she can contribute and feel good about. Lots of laughter, no pressure, and a level playing field help create a safe place to begin. The learners are drawn in. They're having fun. They want more. Bridge building doesn't have to be backbreaking work, after all.

A cautionary note: It's tempting to start believing that the stuff of concrete lessons is what's important. There's nothing magical about the concrete objects alone. When it comes to meaningful instruction, it is never really about stuff; it's about *thinking* and *talking* and *learning*. These concrete ideas simply give us a way in to the hearts and minds of our students.

Concrete Quotes

Approaching learning in a concrete way is nothing new. Reflect on these quotes as you consider incorporating concrete experiences for your students into your lessons.

Children are safe within the confines of something concrete.

　　—Georgia Heard, poet and author

The changing of a vague difficulty into a specific, concrete form is a very essential element in thinking.

　　—J. P. Morgan, financier

We are all hungry and thirsty for concrete images.
   —*Salvador Dali, painter*

From past experience we know that the act of transferring newly
learned ideas into a concrete symbol demands a high level of
intellectual reflection and entails a much deeper engagement
with theory.
   —*Mem Fox, author*

Metacognition
It's the Thought That Counts

 first encountered the concept of metacognition as an eighteen-year-old college student at Miami University of Ohio. In my educational psychology text I read how John Flavell used the term in the 1970s; he believed we were capable of monitoring our thoughts, of thinking about our thinking. As my professor explained this concept, I immediately thought, "Wow! I do this! I think about my own thinking all the time! I just didn't know what to call it." I was surprised to learn that researchers had studied metacognition and were examining the implications for teaching and learning. It's an amazing sensation when you discover that the world knows about something that had heretofore belonged solely to you!

I see it happen with kids. I introduce metacognition to my students, and as we talk, kids start to grin and nod. Many of them already *know*. We're noticing and naming our thinking. Maybe they aren't yet metacognitive about their *reading*, but that's where I come in, providing opportunities for practice.

I don't know how to teach thinking strategies unless I begin with metacognition. Taking time to explore metacognition sets a foundation on which to build. In making kids aware of how they think about their own thinking, I open a channel through which purposeful conversation can flow.

With every group of students I teach, no matter the grade level, no matter the subject area, I spend time noticing, naming, and exploring metacognition. Every conversation thereafter is richer.

Launching Sequence: Metacognition

Many of the ideas in this chapter materialized during lessons with first, third, and fourth graders from Summerside Elementary in Cincinnati. Together we defined metacognition and explored what it could mean to us as readers. I am grateful to Bonnie Frey, Angela Giwer, and Gale Proctor, Summerside teachers, for uniting with the kids and me as we plunged into this unfamiliar territory. Within this launching sequence, you'll see what we learned along the way!

Concrete Experience: The Reading Salad

Materials needed: one large bowl, two small bowls, small red paper squares, small green paper squares, a book you're currently reading outside of school, and one deep picture book, like *Don't Laugh at Me,* by Steve Seskin and Allen Shamblin.

Note: Seskin and Shamblin are songwriters. *Don't Laugh at Me* was actually a song before it was a picture book, recorded by Mark Wills and also by Peter, Paul, and Mary.

I begin by saying, "Kids are very good at pretending. Let's pretend together for a few minutes today. I think you'll like this! Please pretend you are the teacher and I am a student. All of you teachers out there are going to listen as I read. Put on your teacher faces." It is always interesting to see what they do in response. Many kids don solemn expressions.

"Judging from your faces, you've noticed that teachers are very serious when it comes to reading! OK, teachers, concentrate now and listen as I read. I'm going to ask you to evaluate me as a reader." I pick up my challenging text, *Warriors of God,* by James Reston Jr. (2001). "My friend Lesley recommended this book to me. It has four hundred ten pages and contains many difficult words. This is a challenging text for me, but I'll do my best as I read the first paragraph aloud to you." I begin reading with

expression and at an appropriate rate. I pronounce each word correctly and
do not appear to have any trouble whatsoever. I read:

> Early in the twelfth century, in the city of Tovin in northern Armenia close
> to Georgia, there lived an eminent family of Kurds, the master of whose
> house was surnamed Najm ad-Din, which meant "excellent prince and star
> of religion." Najm ad-Din had a boon comrade named Bihruz, a man of
> intelligence and charm, qualities matched only by his bent for trouble.

"All right, teachers. Turn and talk. What do you think about me as a
reader? You'll give me my 'report card' in a few moments."

I eavesdrop as the kids converse. After a minute or so, hands are in the
air. "Gosh, I'm nervous. All of these teachers staring at me! Now for the
moment of truth. What do you think of me as a reader?"

"You're a good reader because you're fast."

"You say all the words right."

"You didn't have to stop to get help."

"Phew! I'm so relieved," I exclaim. "You all think I'm such a great
reader!" I pause and look down. "There's something you don't know about
me, though. Sometimes I can fake people out when I read. Let me explain.
When I was in fourth grade, I used to play a little trick on my teacher, Mrs.
Martin. Would you like to know about it?"

Students are genuinely interested in my story. "Sometimes Mrs. Martin
would ask for a volunteer to read aloud to the class. Guess who would
always raise her hand? You're right—me. I could read aloud with the best
of them. I could pronounce long words and read very fast. My classmates
were impressed! But there was something I wasn't doing, however, something that readers should always do. I wasn't *thinking*. I was just reading the
words like a robot would do. If Mrs. Martin had asked me questions about
what I had read, I wouldn't have been able to give thoughtful answers.

"Guess what!? I was doing this fake kind of reading when I read aloud
to you a moment ago. It sounded good, but the *thinking* was missing. You
can't always tell just from listening to somebody read. Do you know what
I'm talking about? Have you ever done any robot reading or fake reading?"

Kids smile from ear to ear, looking sheepishly at their teacher as if
they're revealing a deep, dark secret. Many are surprised to see their teacher
agreeing that she is one of them! (For more information about fake reading,

see Chapter 1 in Cris Tovani's *I Read It, but I Don't Get It* [2000].) "Turn and talk about your experiences with fake reading." I crouch down to listen in.

"Sometimes I read the words but I don't know what I just read."

"If I don't like the book I just move my finger so it looks like I'm reading."

"Sometimes I think about other stuff while I'm reading, like my friends or my soccer games."

I pull the group back together. "You are amazing! Not only are you honest with each other, but you are metacognitive! You are thinking about your thinking. When I read from *Warriors of God*, I showed you what fake reading can be like. Now I want to model real reading. Real reading is like a tossed salad. Have you noticed the three bowls sitting here on the table beside me? We are going to use these objects to help us understand more about real reading. Notice that the bowls are labeled. The large bowl is labeled 'real reading salad' and the small bowls are labeled 'text' and 'thinking.'

"Just like a tossed salad might be a mixture of lettuce and tomatoes, reading salad is a mixture of text and thinking. Inside the two smaller

Figure 2–1 *Ingredients for reading salad*

bowls there are little cards. In the text bowl there are red cards that say 'text.' These are like tomatoes! In the thinking bowl there are green cards that say 'thinking.' These are like pieces of lettuce. With your help, we will make reading salad while enjoying a great book! If you don't understand the connections between reading and salad, don't despair. It will become clearer to you momentarily. Just watch me. I'm going to use this book, *Don't Laugh at Me*, as I model real reading. I chose this text because it will really make us think.

"To show you exactly how real reading works, I'm going to do something that will make me look kind of funny. I will point to the text when I am reading from the text; I will point to my head when I am thinking. That way you'll be able to see the difference between my reading and my thinking. At the same time that is going on, we'll be making salad. Jack, will you be in charge of the tomato bowl—I mean the text bowl? Bridgette, will you handle the lettuce bowl—I mean the thinking bowl? Every time I point to the text, Jack will drop a text card into the big salad bowl. Whenever I point to my head, Bridgette will place a green thinking card into the salad. Right before your eyes you will see what real reading is all about!"

As I begin to read, Jack and Bridgette are in front of the group, ready to do their jobs. Here's how it goes:

I point to the text and read from the front cover. *"Don't Laugh at Me."* Jack drops in a red text card.

I point to my head. "I'm thinking that this book is going to be about kids who make fun of other kids. I hate when that happens." *Bridgette drops in a green thinking card.*

I point to the text and read from the first page. "I'm a little boy with glasses, the one they call a geek." *Jack drops in a text card.*

I point to my head. "Why did they call this boy a geek? My daughter Blythe wears glasses. I would be so angry if someone called her a geek! Just because you wear glasses doesn't make you weird." *Bridgette drops in a thinking card.*

I point to the text. "A little girl who never smiles 'cause I've got braces on my teeth. And I know how it feels to cry myself to sleep." *A text card is dropped into the large bowl.*

I point to my head. "I can barely stand to hear about kids who cry themselves to sleep. I wonder if kids make fun of this girl while she's in the cafeteria? Or maybe while she's riding the bus?" *A thinking card goes into the large bowl.*

I continue modeling this pattern of text–thinking–text–thinking until I reach the midpoint of the book. Then I commend Jack and Bridgette for their excellent work and release them back to the group. I ask the children to turn and talk for a moment, to reflect on what they've just seen. After a couple of minutes, I say, "So what are you thinking now?"

"Reading is a pattern of text and thinking."

"When you think while you read, it makes it more interesting."

"I get the part about the salad now, but I didn't at first."

"You have to go a little slower when you think and read at the same time."

"So interesting," I say. "Let's get back to the book. Only this time *you* will do the thinking! I will continue pointing to the text when I'm reading the text. I will drop in a red text card each time I read. But when it's time for thinking, I'll ask some of *you* to share what is going on inside *your* heads. If you share, you will come up and drop a green thinking card into our reading salad." For every page of text, several kids share their thinking. The green cards are being added at a much faster rate than the red ones.

"There's more green in here than red," Emma points out as she tosses the salad.

"That's how it's supposed to be," Hillary adds.

"Say more about that," I prompt.

She responds without hesitation. "You're *supposed* to have more thinking than you do text. When you read a book, your thinking takes up way more space than the words on the page." I couldn't have said it better myself!

"Now we've been doing *real* reading. No more of that fake stuff for us. Our reading salad symbolizes what good reading is made of. The two special ingredients are text and thinking. It's sort of weird, isn't it? We've been *thinking* about our *thinking*! There's a name for that: metacognition. In the days to come, we will be learning more about metacognition and what it means to think about thinking."

Sensory Exercises: Metacognition

When Books and Brains Collide

Sometimes kids have to see it to believe it. The Reading Salad experience creates a mental picture for students that they won't soon forget, but it's also helpful to provide a graphic representation of metacognition, one that will reinforce what they have experienced. It's great to start with a Venn diagram, one of the most popular graphic organizers since its introduction in 1881! Most kids are introduced to the Venn in kindergarten or first grade, usually in math or reading.

Note: If your students are not familiar with the Venn diagram, or if they need a refresher, consider providing them with a concrete experience. Overlap hula hoops on the classroom floor to show the organization of the Venn, with kids actually stepping in and out of the circles. Playground jump ropes can be easily formed into a Venn as well.

Teachers sometimes use creative versions of the Venn diagram to make the graphic organizer more meaningful. The Venn diagram I use to support instruction about metacognition overlaps a book shape with a head shape, illustrating the intersection of text and thinking. (See Figure 2–2.)

I sketch this unusual Venn on a piece of chart paper, intentionally leaving it void of text. I want to mix a lot of purposeful talk with the creation of this anchor chart.

"Metacognition. Thinking about your thinking. Reading salad. Ingredients for real reading. Turn and talk about these things. What do they mean to you?" This turn-and-talk session connects us with prior instruction. It also gives the students a chance to express any new thinking they've generated since the previous lesson.

"We all learn in different ways. Take metacognition, for example. For some of you, simply *hearing* about metacognition helps you understand. However, many of you need to *experience* it. That's why we made reading salad. You dropped in the text and thinking cards and actually observed the creation of the salad as your thinking progressed. Let's approach metacognition from another angle. Many of us in this room, myself included, are visual learners. We like to see words and information arranged in graphic organizers. Let's use this Venn diagram to sort out what we've learned about thinking. Instead of two circles overlapping,

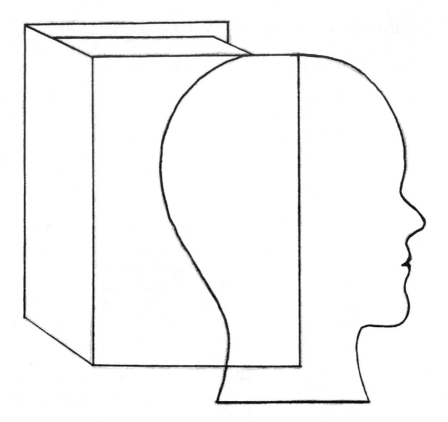

Figure 2–2 *Graphic organizer for real reading*

we'll intersect a book and a head! Turn and talk about how you think this diagram will help us."

Moments later we begin with the left side of the Venn. "I'm going to write in this area first. As I write, please feel free to infer aloud. You might predict what I am going to write even before I write it!" Slowly I write "Text" and then "What the author has to say." The kids finish before I do, using their previous learning to fuel their predictions.

"Now for the right side of the Venn." I write "Thinking" and then "What's going on in my head," with the kids inferring aloud as I write. "Hmmm, 'text' is on one side, and 'thinking' is on the other. We mix them together in the middle and what do we get?"

"Real reading!" echoes across the room. Although the noise level exceeds my comfort zone a bit, the kids are beginning to understand! (See Figure 2–3.)

Figure 2–3 *Our anchor chart for real reading*

"Maybe we should give this chart a title. Since math really makes sense to some of you, let's use a mathematical equation." Usually a couple of kids are ahead of me on this one. "Text plus thinking equals real reading. Perfect! Is it all making sense now? The salad, the Venn diagram, the math equation? What is most meaningful to you? Turn and talk." I give the kids a few minutes to share.

"Let's link another important concept to our chart: metacognition. When we think about this process of real reading, that *is* metacognition. We are thinking about our thinking. Let's post this chart in a prominent place to encourage future thinking. Over the next few days we will exercise metacognition in interesting ways, extending what we've already learned."

Over the years, kids have made some thoughtful suggestions for this lesson. One student encouraged me to place a heart in the center of the Venn, since mixing in your thinking creates a love for reading. Another idea was to provide students with individual Venn diagrams for their notebooks. A fifth-grade student actually created one during a lesson, gave it to me, and requested copies for his classmates! Since then, I've found it helpful to give the students their own blank Venn after the lesson, encouraging them to organize their thinking from the past couple of days. Some kids duplicate the class chart on the wall, while others personalize their text a bit. Either way, it's yet another concrete block in this bridge we're building. How it pays to listen to kids; they can make us so much better at what we do!

The Thought Bubble (aka How to Get Inside Your Teacher's Head)

My husband, Miles, an elementary school art teacher, loves to teach cartooning. To make cartoons more interesting and sophisticated, Miles encourages kids to use thought bubbles. He showcases Charles Schultz as the mentor cartoonist; Schultz's Snoopy character has been thinking aloud for us since the 1950s. Creating the text inside a thought bubble is a metacognitive exercise of sorts. The text in the thought bubble is not really the character's thinking; it's the artist's thinking *about* the character's thinking. To make things even more interesting, the reader comes along to enjoy the cartoon and thinks about the character's thinking, which is actually the artist's thinking. Gives you a scholarly excuse to read the funny pages, doesn't it? Anyway, using thought bubbles gives kids the opportunity to think about thinking.

The thought bubble I use to support the study of metacognition is *not* comic strip sized. It is two feet wide, constructed of poster board! My purpose in using this overgrown thought bubble is to explicitly demonstrate how proficient readers think while they are reading and to assure students that the little voice they hear inside their heads does not mean they are crazy. It's the "conversation voice," as Tovani (2000, 42) calls it, the voice that merges with the text.

Because I want to model the process for the students before they participate, I enlist the help of another teacher to take on the reader's role. I could use most any text, but I tend to use nonfiction for this exercise. I want to make it undeniably clear that readers need to think while reading *anything*, not just fiction. I tell the students that they are going to have the experience of a lifetime, getting into the mind of a teacher! What kid hasn't wondered what goes on inside a teacher's brain? I hold up the giant thought bubble and stand next to the reader. Since many kids are familiar with the function of thought bubbles from cartoons, they understand what's happening right away.

As you can see in Figure 2–4, the reader is seated and the thinker is standing alongside with her head poking through the thought bubble, *Laugh-In* style (if you were born after the 1960s, ask someone). Progress is made as the reader reads the text and the thinker thinks aloud as if they were one and the same person. Here's an example using *Animals Asleep*, by Sneed B. Collard III (2004).

READER: *Animals Asleep,* by Sneed B. Collard III, illustrated by Anik McGrory.

THINKER: Hmmm, this book must be about the sleeping patterns of animals. I hardly know anything about that. This will be interesting!

READER: Most of us need sleep.

Figure 2–4 *Mitch and Megan model reading and thinking*

THINKER: I know I do. I didn't get quite enough last night as a matter of fact.

READER: Whether it's a snooze...

THINKER: I think a *snooze* is another word for *nap*; maybe the author will tell me.

READER: Orangutans live in the rain forests of Southeast Asia. They are closely related to humans and are Earth's largest tree-dwelling animals. An orangutan spends most of its day looking for fruits and other food, but it pauses now and then for a snooze in the trees. Often, before each nap—and before turning in for the night—it weaves a comfortable sleeping nest of branches and leaves.

THINKER: Yes! A snooze *is* like a nap. Sounds like a great life to me...spending your day eating and napping! I wonder what the sleeping nest really looks like.

The teacher and I continue our reading-thinking pattern until about halfway through the book, when we stop to invite others to assume the roles of reader and thinker. Of course there are usually some students who have been *dying* to be the thinker since the beginning of the lesson. An introverted child, however, might be encouraged to be the reader, since that role is scripted. No matter how you decide to use this lesson, kids are sure to enjoy and remember getting inside their teacher's brain for a little while, and what it actually *looks* like to think while you're reading.

Color Cards

With one visit to a hardware store you can come away with a class set of materials that will help kids express their thinking. Paint chip cards, or color cards, as my local store calls them, are free for the asking and can be a meaningful concrete model of thinking. The color gradients can clearly represent the levels of a reader's understanding. While reading challenging text, for example, one's understanding might oscillate from clear to foggy to anywhere in between. Students can actually touch a color card to indicate the clarity of their understanding of text, compelling them to think about their thinking. (See Figure 2–5.)

When I confer with readers, they like to *show* me their level of understanding by using a card as a model. A couple of the teachers I work with have assembled collections of color cards and placed them in accessible

Figure 2–5 *Sierra uses a color card while reading*

spots. I've seen kids use color cards when discussing their social studies and science texts, and even when expressing understanding of a math problem. Some students even name the different shades as they think about their thinking. (See Figure 2–6.)

As an added benefit, the use of color cards is a concrete way to introduce rubrics!

Wordless Books: A Picture Is Worth a Thousand Thoughts

When a strategy or concept has been launched and students have experienced it in several ways, it's time to travel on. Wordless picture books are the ticket. The depth and quality of wordless books have never been better. At my favorite bookstore the wordless books have achieved special status: a shelf to call their own. When we *read* a wordless book, it's easy to be aware of our own thinking. No text is present to get in our way!

Figure 2–6 *A student-labeled color card*

Almost any wordless book will encourage thinking about thinking. My favorite, however, is *The Red Book*, by Barbara Lehman (2004). Inside the dust jacket, Lehman even draws a picture of herself drawing a picture of herself! This book was meant for metacognition. Each page demands high-level thinking, with the experiences of two characters intertwining in intricate ways.

Consider partnering students with a wordless book, providing each pair with a few simple "thinking stems" to support their dialogue. (See Figure 2–7.) Encourage students to progress slowly through the book, talking about their thinking on every page. Even though students aren't reading *text*, they are reading the illustrations, practicing metacognition with a book in their hands.

When I stop to think about *my* thinking, I realize that this launching sequence has taken us from tossed salad to thought bubbles to *books*. We sure ended up in the right place!

Quotes About Thinking to Get Kids Talking!

Post these quotes in your classroom as you investigate metacognition. Consider opening or closing lessons with these quotations, inviting students to turn and talk. The second-grade students in Figure 2–8 discussed quotes written on sentence strips at the end of a strategy study.

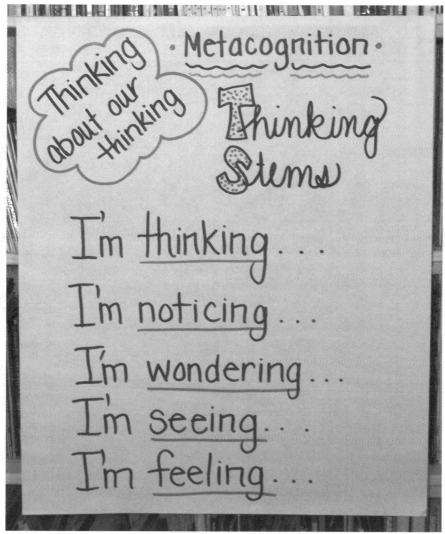

Figure 2–7 *Thinking stems for metacognition*

When the mind is thinking it is talking to itself.
   —*Plato, philosopher*

Thinking is the hardest work there is, which is probably the reason why so few engage in it.
   —*Henry Ford, industrialist*

Figure 2–8 *Kelsey and Brandon discuss a quotation.*

No brain is stronger than its weakest think.

—*Thomas L. Masson, author*

Learning without thought is labor lost.

—*Confucius, philosopher*

A library is thought in cold storage.

—*Herbert Samuel, politician*

Thinking is only a process of talking to yourself.

—*author unknown*

A moment's thinking is an hour in words.

—*Thomas Hood, poet*

Readers are plentiful, thinkers are rare.

—*Harriet Martineau, writer and philosopher*

Time for Text: Metacognition

Check out these resources for next-step lesson ideas about thinking!

Cunningham, Andie, and Ruth Shagoury. 2005. *Starting with Comprehension*. Portland, ME: Stenhouse. See pages 23–30, "Teaching How to Think About Thinking."

Harvey, Stephanie, and Anne Goudvis. 2005. *The Comprehension Toolkit*. Portsmouth, NH: Heinemann. See Strategy Cluster Book 1, *Monitor Comprehension*.

Oczkus, Lori. 2004. *Super 6 Comprehension Strategies*. Norwood, MA: Christopher-Gordon. See Chapter 6, "Monitoring Comprehension."

Zimmermann, Susan, and Chryse Hutchins. 2003. *7 Keys to Comprehension*. New York: Three Rivers. See Chapter 7, "Cultivating Awareness."

Schema

Your Own World Wide Web

'm not exactly crazy about spiders. I know, I know, they are helpful little things and if they weren't around bugs would overtake the world. I understand. But that doesn't mean I want them in my house. Or in my car. No, I'm not the type to scream at the sight of a spider, but if I spot one on the ceiling, I won't relax until those eight legs are reunited with the great outdoors!

Spider *webs* are a different story. They're magical. I gaze at them and think about the time and genius it took to create such masterpieces, works of art that go mainly unnoticed. What fascinates me is that these almost invisible connections link seemingly unrelated objects together. By early autumn in Ohio, you'll discover that almost everything outside is webbed together if you stop to notice. As I step onto my deck on an October morning, I spy a silvery network that seems to go on forever. My wrought-iron patio table is laced to its chairs, and another web joins my flower box of impatiens to the birdbath. Upon closer inspection, I become aware of the debris trapped in the intricate design: tiny leaves, flyaway seeds, unfortunate moths. This collection is a plain history of the passing of time for one spider.

One warm autumn afternoon I presented these familiar images to a group of Ohio third graders and then invited them to turn and talk about how spider webs are like thinking. Prepare to be impressed!

- Flies stick in spider webs. Memories stick in brains.
- My thinking is like a web. It's a net that catches anything I see or hear.

■ Sometimes a web catches things that a spider wants, sometimes things he doesn't want. That's like me. Sometimes I think of good memories and I want to remember them. But other times I try to forget things I don't want to think about.

■ The web in my brain changes with each new experience I have.

■ A spider can make a web fit into whatever space it has. I can fit my thinking into any time I have.

■ Spider webs connect trees and weeds. My thinking connects my brain to books.

■ My thinking is my own World Wide Web!

What significant connections these kids constructed! How were eight- and nine-year-olds able to do this? First of all, simply having kids turn and talk deserves some credit. If left to think of connections on their own, many kids would lose confidence and shut down. With a friend, everything's easier. Most importantly, however, these kids were able to connect because they have *schema* for spider webs. Most of these kids have touched, examined, and appreciated webs since their first walks outside years ago. They didn't have to take time to get to know the properties of spider webs; that was already embedded. Having schema allows our thinking to go deeper, faster. Just think of the implications for everything we teach. Using what kids already know can help us do what we do better. We just need to invite them to make meaningful connections, and they will rise to meet us.

Note: I often use the word *schema* with my students; I appreciate how concise and exact the term is. My students are invited to use the terms *background knowledge* and *prior knowledge* as well. We fuse all of that language together as we learn to use our connections to deepen our comprehension.

I learned about the value of prior knowledge the hard way. In my first teaching position I used a basal reader that told me to be sure to tap the students' background knowledge prior to reading each selection. The problem was I didn't know how.

My students often gave dry, dispassionate responses without emotion or opinion. I thought that because many of them had never stepped outside the boundaries of the county in which they lived, they were giving me all they had to give. I became so very frustrated trying to make connections for my students, taking that on as my responsibility. I spent time trying to forge inauthentic links between kids and text, when I could have been teaching kids how to make meaningful connections of their own. Case in point: One of the selections in my literature anthology was "Kyo's Secret" by Deborah Davis, the story of an Alaskan boy who fears for the safety of a seal. This story seemed about as far away from our day-to-day Ohio lives as is possible. I can still see the faces of my midwestern students as they read the words from the text. They were word calling. They were page turning. They could answer the four questions at the end of the story. But they never really felt Kyo's fear or loss. For most of my students, the entire reading experience was shallow and insignificant. Just another assignment.

I've learned that whenever my students are just going through the motions, I should look for an error in *my* belief system or in *my* approach. When it came to prior knowledge, I was trying to forge connections that were not authentic, believing that because my students were not well traveled, they couldn't do it on their own. Wrong. How shallow to think that geographic location is the only way to connect to a text! Truth be told, my students had all they needed to connect with Kyo and his Alaskan life. They had experienced friendship, grief, and fear just like any other human on the planet. I was looking at connecting to the text in a dry, superficial way, not inviting my students to connect at the deep emotional level that they were capable of.

This chapter shows how my thinking has changed since my early days in the classroom, now valuing most what the *reader* brings to the table.

Launching Sequence: Schema
Concrete Experience: The Schema Roller

Materials needed: one lint roller (the kind with the sticky tear-off sheets) and several one-by-two-inch slips of lightweight paper

"You are so incredibly special. There has never been anyone like you and there never will be again. Turn and talk for a moment about what it is exactly that makes you so unique."

Listening in, I hear mention of hair type, skin color, first names, and favorite foods. "You're off to a good start. What you look like and what your name is certainly make you special. But let's go deeper than that. What is it that makes you different on the inside? Turn and talk." I give them a little bit longer this time, making sure they have enough time to dig down deep.

"So what are you thinking? What is it really that makes you *you*?" The kids have a lot of good ideas.

- I'm the only one who has my parents and my family, well, except for my brother.

- My family has gone to Lake Erie three times and most of the kids I know have never been there.

- I have spent a lot of time in the kitchen at a big hotel since my grandma is the chef there. I know a lot about cooking.

- We moved here last year, so I have had different teachers than anyone else in this class and I learned different things at my old school.

- I am patient with kids who have special needs since my sister has Down's syndrome.

"Now you're getting there! You are identifying thoughts, experiences, and feelings that make you unique. Lots of other people might have a similar kind of hair and the same color eyes, but no one else has experienced life in just the way you have. We might say your background or prior knowledge is different from anyone else's. Or we could call this your schema. Your schema is yours and yours alone."

I place a large lint roller on top of the table. "Let me show you what schema is like. Pretend with me for a moment that this lint roller is my brain! My brain is ready to stick to whatever it comes in contact with. On these little slips of paper, I've written down some things that have stuck to my brain through the years. I have included some thoughts, feelings, experiences, relationships, and passions.

"Here's what I wrote down: I love the tastes of chocolate and coffee mixed together. I have visited Mammoth Cave National Park at least five times. My mom used to own a hair salon. I spend hours watching my daughter Brynne do gymnastics. Tornados scare me. Bluegrass music puts me in a good mood."

I sprinkle the papers across the table; then I take the sticky roller and roll it over them. "Over the course of my life, I've picked up millions of experiences, thoughts, and feelings and they're all rolled together in my brain. All of these things together constitute my schema. I guess we could say this is a schema roller instead of a sticky roller!"

I tear off my schema sheet and offer the roller to a student, who follows my lead and models her schema for the class. She jots down some pieces of her past on a few small scraps of paper and then gathers them up with the sticky roller. Of course everyone else wants a chance, so we return to our tables to capture bits of our past on the paper slips, taking turns creating our schema sheets. I use this concrete reminder to help kids notice and name prior knowledge; then I move along to sensory experiences to show how our schema helps us as thinkers.

Sensory Exercises: Schema

The One-Minute Schema Determiner

Many kids need proof that a strategy will really help them. To prove the value of schema to my students, I often use the One-Minute Schema Determiner, for lack of a better name. On a large piece of chart paper I make a huge letter *T*, creating an instant graphic organizer. I tell the students that in just a moment I am going to write a topic on the top left line of the T-chart. They will have thirty seconds to call out their thoughts, feelings, opinions, and experiences with regard to the topic. I designate one student as the timer and then write "Kings Island" on the paper. (Kings Island is a local amusement park.) As I write those two words, kids get noisy. Someone cheers. I hear laughter and see smiling faces. "Go!" I shout. For the next thirty seconds, the classroom is alive with expressions of joy, names of rides and foods, mention of family members and friends. I have to stop them at the end of thirty seconds, but they could go on and on.

I now switch my attention to the right side of the chart. I tell the students we are going to repeat this same exercise, again with thirty seconds on the clock. Instead of Kings Island, I'll choose a new topic, however. I deliberately choose something I think will be unfamiliar to my midwestern students. I write "Immokalee," and then we start the timer. "Call out your thoughts, emotions, and opinions," I ask.

For the first three seconds, the classroom is silent. Then a boy in the back of the room says, "What is that?" I write down his question.

"Sounds like broccoli."

"It has four syllables."

"Is it a girl's name?"

"Did you make it up, Mrs. McGregor?"

Without schema, their comments quickly turn to questions and word observation. Thirty seconds expires and I step back from the chart. "Wow. We did the same thing on both sides of our T-chart, but it sure seemed different the first time than the second. Let's stop to be metacognitive. What was your thinking like when you saw the topic Kings Island?"

- I had so much thinking, I couldn't get it all out.

- I felt happy about my memories from last summer.

- I had a lot to say. I didn't have enough time.

- Those two words made me feel like I was at Kings Island again.

"I noticed that you were energized as soon as you saw the topic! I didn't even have to say anything. You filled the thirty seconds with your knowledge, opinions, and firsthand experiences. You were confident and didn't hesitate to share your thinking.

"Now reflect on the second half of the chart. Think about your thinking here. What was going on in your mind when you saw the topic Immokalee?"

- I didn't have anything to say.

- My mind was blank.

- I was full of questions and guesses.

- I wondered if it was a trick.

"I noticed that you were suddenly quiet and unsure. No laughter or chatter. When someone did find the courage to speak up, it was with a questioning tone in his voice. Only a few people chose to speak. What accounts for the difference in the first column and the second column?

Why such a different reaction to the two topics? Turn and talk." I circulate, listening in.

- I've been to Kings Island a bunch of times. I've never even heard of that other place. I have a lot to say about a place if I've been there before.

- My feelings are strong about Kings Island. I know what it's like. I don't have any feelings one way or another about Immokalee.

- I have memories from one and not the other.

- I didn't want to say anything the second time because I was afraid to be wrong. I shared a lot of thinking about Kings Island because I knew what I was talking about.

"Great. You are being metacognitive about what we just experienced. I can sum it up for you in just one word. Watch this." I take a marker and write "schema" down the left-hand column of the chart. (See Figure 3–1.)

"Schema makes all the difference. It's your feelings, experiences, thoughts, and opinions all wrapped up into one. It's everything you've ever seen, tasted, smelled, felt, or heard. Your schema is you, and no one else has schema just like yours. From the T-chart we just completed, I can tell that many of you have schema for Kings Island. None of you have schema for Immokalee, however, but I do. My parents live in Florida, near the Everglades. There's this little town called Immokalee that isn't too far from where they live. When I passed through that town not long ago, there were children playing out in the streets. They smiled at me through my open car window. The air was heavy with a slight breeze, and I could smell spicy food cooking at the taqueria. I remember wondering what it would be like to teach in a school in this town. I have so many memories of that day. I have schema." I leave our schema determiner chart posted for a long while, reminding us of the importance and power of schema.

The presence of schema increases a reader's feeling of self-confidence and his willingness to take risks. It enables the reader to remember new information, connecting to what is known. In teaching our readers how to access and activate their personal schema, we boost their chances for meaningful interaction with text.

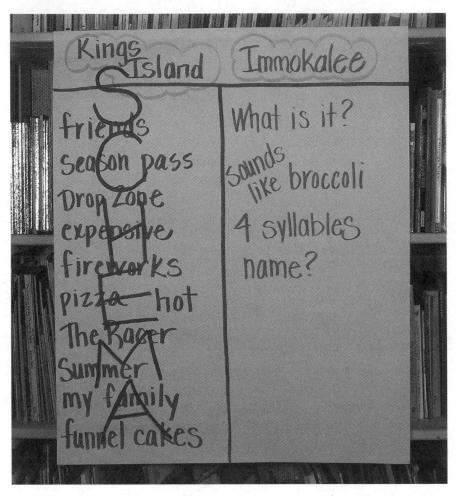

Figure 3–1 *Schema T-chart*

Concentric Circles of Connection: "Rachel Delevoryas"

Now we've noticed and named the strategy of tapping prior knowledge, and we've discovered what a difference it can make to readers. Let's take a look at what kinds of connections readers make. In *Mosaic of Thought*, Ellin Keene and Susan Zimmermann (1997) tell us that connections can emerge in three ways:

- **Text-to-self connections:** when text makes me think of my own life

- **Text-to-text connections:** when a text makes me think of another text (or media of any kind)

- **Text-to-world connections:** when text makes me think of the world around me, maybe a theme or a big idea

Concentric circles are a perfect way to organize these connections.

I want kids to start thinking about the kinds of connections they can make and how these connections make the text come alive. Short, meaningful text always works well when launching a strategy, so I usually look for

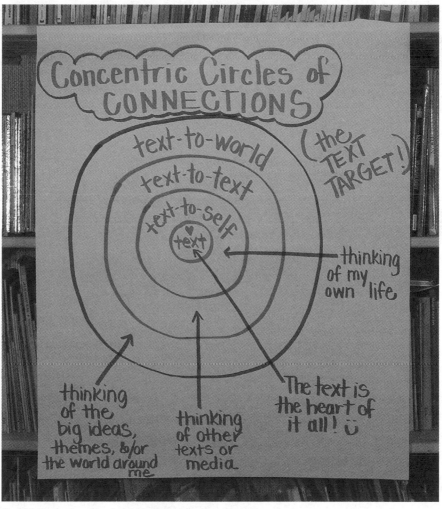

Figure 3–2 *Concentric circles of connection*

songs with lyrics that allow students to practice their strategic thinking. The music serves as a scaffold, allowing kids to organize their thinking with ease. They are freed up to think about their connections. My favorite song to use with this organizer is "Rachel Delevoryas," written and recorded by Randy Stonehill (1992). I've yet to meet a kid who can't make some instant connections to these poignant lyrics.

Note: "Rachel Delevoryas," like most of the songs mentioned in this book, is available from iTunes. For a minimal fee, you can choose to burn a CD of selected songs or download them to your computer or iPod. Visit www.apple.com/itunes/ for more information.

Rachel Delevoryas

by Randy Stonehill

Rachel Delevoryas
With her thick eye glasses and her plain Jane face
Sat beside me in my fifth grade class
Looking so terribly out of place
Rachel played the violin
And classical music was out of style
She couldn't control all her wild brown hair
Her nervous laughter and her awkward smile and
> *It was clear that she'd never be one of us*
> *With her dowdy clothes*
> *And her violin*
> *And a name like Rachel Delevoryas*

But I'd pass by her house in the evening
Going to play with my best friend Ray
And the music floating from her window
Spoke the things that Rachel could never say

Rachel Delevoryas
Was eating her lunch as the boys walked by
"Rachel is ugly" she heard them shout
She sat on the schoolyard bench and cried and
> *It was clear that she'd never be one of us*
> *With her dowdy clothes*
> *And her violin*
> *And a name like Rachel Delevoryas*

And every year the hedge got higher
As it grew around Rachel's house
Like the secret wall inside her
That she built to keep all the heartache out

Rachel Delevoryas
Moved back east with her family
Now she's dressed in a beautiful gown
Standing on stage with the symphony
Rachel plays the violin
But every night when the lights go down
I wonder if she still remembers those days
And cruel little boys in this one horse town and
    It was clear that she'd never be one of us
    With her dowdy clothes and her violin
    And a name like Rachel Delevoryas
    A name like Rachel Delevoryas

© 1992 Stonehillian Music (Amin. by Word Music, LLC) Word Music, LLC. All rights reserved. Used by permission.

After experiencing this tender song, my students always have earnest conversations with each other. Trey is reminded of the situation on his bus route where kids pick on a certain boy every afternoon. Brandi remembers *Don't Laugh at Me*, and mentions that she can't stop thinking about how unfair the world can be. Jazlyn thinks about how people always seem to tease those who are different. Many students choose to hold their thinking on sticky notes as they talk.

I direct attention to the concentric circles organizer, pointing out how the organizer will support us as we think about our thinking. I invite students to place their sticky notes on the chart in the appropriate circle. We watch as the circles fill with connections, noticing how many text-to-self notes we have created. I suggest that maybe we're more comfortable making text-to-self connections than other types, but one very thoughtful student says that the text is partly responsible for that: the lyrics of "Rachel Delevoryas" remind us of so much from our own lives. The music and the organizer support my students as they explore making connections, learning how our schema can make text intense, rich, and life changing.

When I devote enough time to student-to-student talk, strong themes always emerge. It's almost as if noticing and naming the strategy leads us to the bigger, deeper ideas that are even more meaningful. Case in point: I recently observed Mike Laehr's fourth graders at Clough Pike Elementary as they listened to "Rachel" for the first time. Many kids closed their eyes as they listened, while others chose to sketch along in a lyric booklet that Mike had created. (See Figure 3–3.)

As the song played, I could see the connections surface on each face: pain when it hit too close to home, relief as Rachel's happy ending was revealed. Whenever he sensed his students were about to burst with ideas, Mike paused the song and listened in while the kids conferred. At first, the talk was filled with connections, but it wasn't long before deeper, more significant issues rose to the top. Students aired opinions and concerns about bullying, racism, and social inequality while taking notes and drawing in their lyric booklets. Mike doesn't teach thinking strategies for the sake of the strategies themselves. It is always about themes, about meaning, about significance.

I am convinced that songs reach more deeply into the hearts of our students than we might ever imagine. Don't stop with "Rachel." There are plenty of songs out there with lyrics that will connect directly to the experiences of your students. Many songwriters compose with this express purpose. Here are a few of my favorites:

- "We're Going to Be Friends," the White Stripes (school and friendship)

- "Popular," Kristin Chenoweth (relationships and social status)

- "Old Blue," the Byrds (loss of a pet)

- "You've Got a Friend in Me," Randy Newman (friendship)

Norman Rockwell: Enduring Connections

Art gives us an effective way to further scaffold strategic thinking. Blending art with thinking and talk is instinctive for kids.

One of America's most prolific storytellers didn't use words. With his right hand, Norman Rockwell painted timeless themes that still evoke emotion and activate the schema of our students. Dozens of his paintings depict

Figure 3–3 *Heidi's thinking about "Rachel Delevoryas"*

the everyday experiences of children, making Rockwell's work an ideal choice for supporting instruction about schema. Art teachers are an excellent resource for prints and reproductions. Calendars, library collections, and the Internet also make it easy to locate pieces that your students will strongly connect to. A few pieces that have worked well for me are *High Dive* (1947), *A Day in the Life of a Boy* (1951), *A Day in the Life of a Girl* (1952), and *Surprise* (*Happy Birthday, Miss Jones*) (1956). Students pair up to examine Rockwell's work and place sticky notes on the edges of the prints. For extra support, students can choose to use the thinking stems I've posted. (See Figure 3–4.)

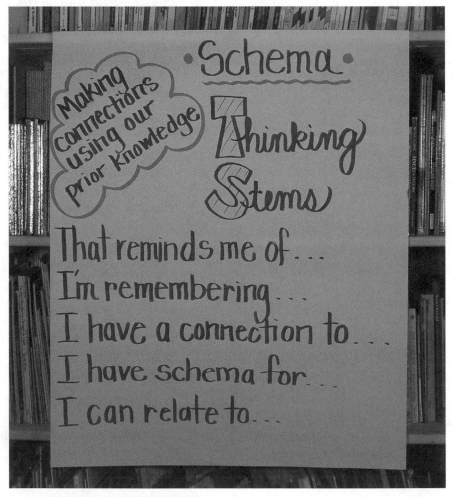

Figure 3–4 *Thinking stems for schema*

The sticky notes display connections to self, other media, or the world. After a time, I bring the students back to a sharing circle to talk about how their connections promoted deeper understanding of Rockwell's work.

The Wordless Books of Mercer Mayer

Consider using Mercer Mayer's A Boy, a Dog, and a Frog series (Puffin Pied Piper Books) right before jumping into text. Mayer is considered the father of the wordless picture book genre. Recently reissued after thirty-five years, this charming series of six wordless books gives students plenty to connect to! Pairs or small groups can enjoy the frog's antics while making connections to their own life experiences. Make thinking stems available as kids tour these treasures.

Quotes About Schema to Get Kids Talking!

The web of our life is of a mingled yarn, good and ill together.
   —*William Shakespeare, poet and playwright*

There is beauty in tangible memories.
   —*Patricia Polacco, author*

I am a part of all that I have met.
   —*Alfred Lord Tennyson, poet*

We don't accomplish anything in this world alone...and whatever happens is the result of the whole tapestry of one's life and all the weavings of individual threads from one to another that creates something.
   —*Sandra Day O'Connor, Supreme Court justice*

We are all connected to everyone and everything in the universe. Therefore, everything one does as an individual affects the whole. All thoughts, words, images, prayers, blessings, and deeds are listened to by all that is.
   —*Serge Kahili King, author*

Our lives are connected by a thousand invisible threads, and along these sympathetic fibers, our actions run as causes and return to us as results.
—*Herman Melville, author*

When one tugs at a single thing in nature, he finds it attached to the rest of the world.
—*John Muir, conservationist*

The way a book is read—which is to say, the qualities a reader brings to a book—can have as much to do with its worth as anything the author puts into it.
—*Norman Cousins, editor and writer*

Time for Text: Schema

Check out these resources for next-step schema lesson ideas!

Cunningham, Andie, and Ruth Shagoury. 2005. *Starting with Comprehension*. Portland, ME: Stenhouse. See Chapter 3, "Connections and Comprehension."

Harvey, Stephanie, and Anne Goudvis. 2000. *Strategies That Work*. Portland, ME: Stenhouse. See Chapter 6, "Making Connections."

———. 2005. *The Comprehension Toolkit*. Portsmouth, NH: Heinemann. See Strategy Cluster Book 2, *Activate and Connect*.

Hoyt, Linda. 2000. *Snapshots*. Portsmouth, NH: Heinemann. See page 36, "Group Think Aloud/Activating Prior Knowledge," and page 142, "Making Connections."

———. 2002. *Make It Real*. Portsmouth, NH: Heinemann. See Chapter 9, "Prereading Strategies: Building Understanding for Content and Vocabulary."

Miller, Debbie. 2002. *Reading with Meaning*. Portland, ME: Stenhouse. See Chapter 5, "Schema."

Oczkus, Lori. 2004. *Super 6 Comprehension Strategies.* Norwood, MA: Christopher-Gordon. See Chapter 2, "Building Background and Making Connections."

Szymusiak, Karen, and Franki Sibberson. 2001. *Beyond Leveled Books.* Portland, ME: Stenhouse. See pages 20–21, "Mini-Lesson: Using Background Knowledge."

Zimmermann, Susan, and Chryse Hutchins. 2003. *7 Keys to Comprehension.* New York: Three Rivers. See Chapter 3, "Making Connections."

4

Inferring
Not Just Anybody's Guess

1972 Me, in my bell-bottom corduroys, tumbling off the bus after a long day in first grade. Scooby and Shaggy were always there waiting as I stretched out, just three feet from the television. Was this my time for passive TV viewing? No way! From the very moment that the green Mystery Machine van appeared on the screen, I used clues to help me guess the identity of the bad guy. Cartoon watching, or animated inference training? Maybe a combination of both, but I think it's significant that no wild guessing was going on. I always based my inferences on evidence, evidence from the text (script) and the animation. When I relate this story to my students, they always nod in understanding. (See Figure 4–1.)

They know as well as I do how much fun inferring can be! Guessing is a childhood pleasure. Game companies take advantage of this; dozens of "guessing" games can be purchased at your local toy store. We should take a cue and make the most of the enjoyment inferring can bring. Children infer, all the time, every day—but that doesn't necessarily mean they know how to infer with text. When difficult text gets in the way, inferring can become drudgery. So the explicit teaching of inferring is one of the most important things we can give our students. Without it, many students may not experience the exhilaration that inferential thinking can bring. Inferring makes reading fun!

The ability to infer helps us make solid deductions, often in a short amount of time. When you break it down, inferring is really the process of

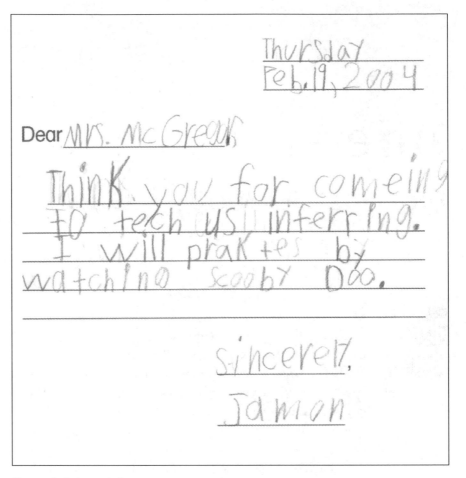

Figure 4–1 *Jamon's letter*

merging your schema with an evidence-based guess. In *Blink*, Malcolm Gladwell (2005) writes about the decisions and judgments that humans make in an instant, sometimes solidly and sometimes with misconceptions. Of course I read this book through the lens of a reading teacher, and it seemed to me a book about the strategy of inferring. Gladwell reminds us that this kind of thinking is "an ability that we can all cultivate"(16). We must remember this. Even those students who think very literally and never seem to read between the lines *can* learn to infer; they just need time and practice.

As a third-grade teacher, I would sometimes feel frustrated when teaching inferring lessons. My students seemed overwhelmed. I knew the ability to infer was crucial: in reading, in test taking, even in life. I think now, however, that I expected my students to do too many new things at once. My instruction combined grasping new language, decoding, and processing challenging text with making solid inferences. Too much, too fast. This chapter reflects the changes in my thinking with regard to teaching inferring, providing a map for doling out responsibility in manageable pieces.

Teaching students to infer can be a load of garbage. No, really. A couple of years ago, I was asked to speak at a school board meeting (a cable-televised session, mind you) to help the board members understand strategy instruction. Besides being a little nervous, I was very excited. What a great opportunity to create awareness and rally support! I wasn't exactly sure how to plan, but I knew right away that I didn't want to present some dull, mind-numbing lecture based on a bunch of overheads with diminutive print. No *bored* board for me. After thinking about it for a couple of days, it hit me: make it concrete! I decided to deliver a brief research-based rationale for the strategies and then get specific, inviting the board members to experience a single strategy in a concrete way. Inferring was the perfect strategy to use; its importance is certain and it is so much fun to practice! I decided to assemble a bag of garbage to help the board members practice inferring. In a small plastic trash bag, I collected a few discarded items from around my house: an empty bottle of vitamin water, an old Ace bandage, a label from a Lean Cuisine frozen dinner, the receipt from my expired pool membership, a couple of airline ticket stubs from the previous December, a past issue of *Consumer Reports*. I asked the board members to make inferences based on the "hard evidence" that I produced from the garbage bag. Let me just say it was a success...and here's how this little experiment with the school board helped me develop a trusted anchor lesson to use with students when launching inferring.

I tell my students I have an interesting story for them, a mystery of sorts. I describe a house on my street that puzzles me. Someone must live there because sometimes lights are turned on, sometimes the garage door is raised, and so on, but I've never actually seen anyone around. (Now this is not a true story...just a story. The kids enjoy the uncertainty, trying to figure out which parts might be true.) I relate how my curiosity has been getting the best of me. How many people live there? How old are they? What are they like? Why are they so private? I exclaim to the students that it is my lucky day: garbage day in my neighborhood! I recount the experience of driving to school that very morning and noticing a small bag of trash at the end of the driveway of the mystery house. I tell them that before I could talk myself out of it, I hopped out of my car, snatched the bag, and then drove away. At this point some of the kids can see where I'm going with this; some know I'm just pulling their leg. Others are concerned that I broke the law (I assure them that I did not). I produce the premeditated bag of trash, telling the students that by examining the evidence, we can make some inferences to help us figure out the mystery of my neighbors. I emphasize that every inference must be directly supported by evidence. I reveal one piece of trash at a time, inviting kids to turn and talk about what they can infer. I post the inferring stems to aid students as they express their thinking. (See Figure 4–2.)

Here are some of the most common inferences I hear:

- **Bottle of vitamin water:** These people must care about their health. They must have some extra money because that stuff is expensive. You can drink water for free if you want to.

- **Old Ace bandage:** I'm thinking someone got hurt while exercising. Maybe they are trying to get in shape. They threw it away so they must be feeling better.

- **Label from a Lean Cuisine dinner:** I infer that a woman lives in this house because my mom and my aunts eat those kinds of dinners. I'm thinking someone either wants to stay healthy or they want to lose weight.

- **Receipt from pool membership:** I infer that these people want to eat healthy so they can look good at the pool each summer. This must be an active family.

- **Airline tickets:** This family has enough money to go on trips and to fly in an airplane. They probably have jobs. Since they flew to Florida during the holidays, it's likely that they have family or friends that live there.

- ***Consumer Reports* magazine:** These people must care about getting a good value. Maybe they like to read, especially magazines.

Together with their talk partners, kids create a profile of the mystery family, citing their evidence along the way. One class even created a court-

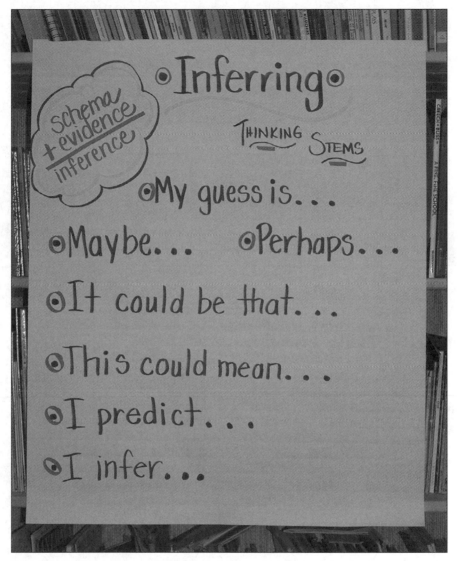

Figure 4–2 *Thinking stems for inferring*

room-style exhibit table, complete with inferences written on index cards that accompanied each item.

This enjoyable exercise is effective with students of all ages. Kids refer to this memorable anchor lesson over and over again as we deepen our study of inferring.

Launching Sequence: Inferring
Concrete Experience: Shoes

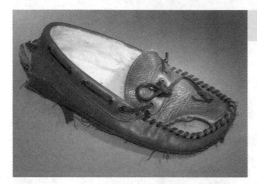

Materials needed: an interesting shoe

Everybody has schema for shoes; they are part of our everyday lives. The shoe schema our students bring to school is quite diverse, however. I have taught students whose new leather Nikes were without a scuff. I have taught many more students, though, whose soles were coming loose and whose laces were soiled and broken. "Mama always said you could tell an awful lot about a person by their shoes." Forrest Gump's mama was right. Shoes have a story to tell if we'll only listen. This is why shoes are a perfect concrete item to use to launch the teaching of inferring. Using shoes to introduce inferring has worked for me again and again!

I always begin with my husband Miles' house slippers. He ordered this pair of leather slippers from the Eddie Bauer catalog about twelve years ago. Don't mistakenly visualize a nice, well-cared for pair of shoes. No. These slippers have been worn to and from the mailbox, they have had kittens sleep in their fleece linings, and their leather laces have not been tied since the 1990s. To say that Miles has gotten his money's worth out of these things is a total understatement. Maybe you even have schema for shoes like these. Anyway, I like to draw my students in close and pull one of these decrepit slippers out of a grocery bag. After the groans subside, I ask the students to think about the person to whom this shoe might belong. As the students pass the slipper around, touching, viewing, even smelling it along the way, they immediately begin to make inferences and collect evidence.

The students are quick to infer: it belongs to someone who likes to relax, someone who has a pet, someone who hates going shoe shopping. I quickly chart as many of these inferences as I can, commending the students for their ability to infer. It usually doesn't take very long to gather a dozen inferences, but we are only halfway home at this point. One request comes from me now: "Cite your evidence!" Just like all of us, kids often jump to conclusions without linking them to something solid. I remind my students that inferences without evidence are just unsubstantiated claims. I want these thinkers to become reflective and metacognitive, always striving to support their thinking. Sometimes this part of the chart is not completed so quickly. This column is excellent practice for what is to come, however, since I will soon be asking them to revisit text to pinpoint supporting evidence.

For every inference written on our chart, we cite the evidence that led us down this path of thinking in the first place. I write the evidence on the right side of the paper, taking time to link the inference and the evidence with brightly colored arrows—just another way to accentuate the link between the two. (See Figure 4–3.)

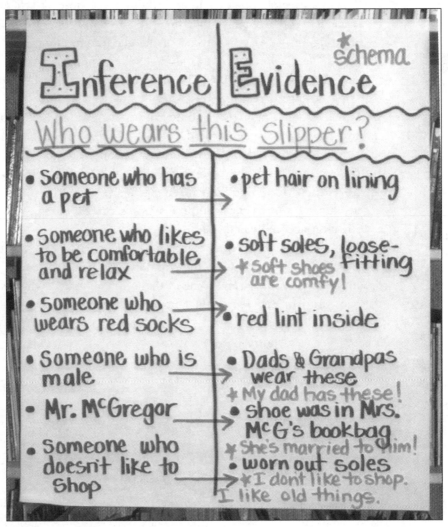

Figure 4–3 *Inferring with Mr. McGregor's slipper*

Some evidence is easy to cite. Consider the pet hair clinging to the slipper's fleece lining. Inference: A pet owner wears this shoe. Evidence? Pet hair on the fleece lining. However, other evidence can be elusive, based more in our schema than in something physical. Here's an example. There is usually a student who will say, "My uncle has slippers like those," or "I saw those slippers in the men's department at Sears." When I first started teaching this lesson, I wasn't prepared for this dilemma. It wasn't as cut-and-dried as I wanted it to be (isn't that always the way!). Never fear; one group of thoughtful students helped me understand. Fourth-grader Tatum said, "Mrs. McG, we really shouldn't infer without a big dose of schema mixed in." Together we created a formula that organized our thinking about inferences. (See Figure 4–4.) We posted it in the classroom, along with the equation from *The Comprehension Toolkit* (Harvey and Goudvis 2005) for future reference. As I jotted down Tatum's words, I left that classroom knowing who the experts really were!

So what? I brought in some grungy slippers and made another chart for the already overcrowded wall. True, but so much more was achieved. My students now know what an inference is. They know the importance of citing evidence. They have language in place that supports their thinking about inferring. Most of all, they feel successful in attempting this crucial comprehension strategy, having fun all the while. Mission accomplished.

Inferring and concrete objects accompany each other wonderfully. How worthwhile to get to know the world around us while practicing inferential thinking! Consider using some of the following objects or sets of objects to help your students secure the language of inferring:

- a shoehorn

- a crumber from a fancy restaurant

- a biscuit cutter

- a garlic press

- printer's dies

- an eight-track tape

- a brayer (ask an art teacher)

- a pitch pipe or tuning fork (ask a music teacher)

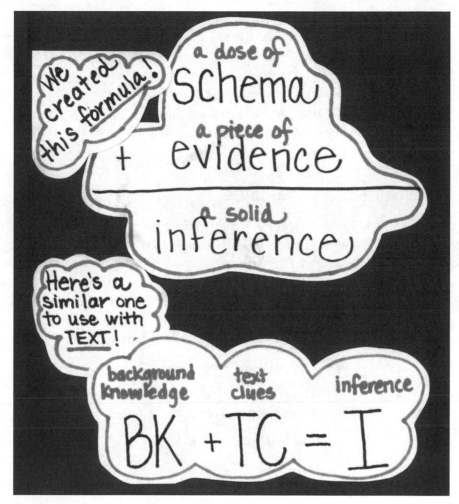

Figure 4–4 *Formulas for inferring*

Sensory Exercises: Inferring

Why You've Been Saving Those Old Magazines!

Thinkers use every clue available to make sense of their world. Here's a simple way to launch that practice. Dust off that old stack of magazines you've been saving for just the right lesson. Tear out advertisements that might seem interesting to children: ads with pets, families, sports, or entertainment. Remove the entire page from the magazine. What item could you cover or cut out that would force the viewer to infer? You can cut out the featured object or, better yet, cover it with a paper flap so that kids can confirm their thinking after inferring. Create enough of these so that pairs can work together. Invite students to examine the evidence, searching for clues to help them infer what the missing item could be. Supported by visual evidence, students can list inferences on sticky notes and place them on the perimeter of the page. For more practice, students can trade pictures again and again.

Listen Between the Lines

Many songs contain lyrics with strong symbolism and layers of meaning. Allowing students to listen to these songs and use thinking stems as they discuss inferences is an enjoyable way to support kids as they become more skilled. The possibilities are endless; try searching your local library or your personal music collection. Some of my favorites are

- "Cat's in the Cradle," Harry Chapin

- "Day Is Done," Peter, Paul, and Mary

- "Halley Came to Jackson," Mary Chapin Carpenter (accompanying picture book available)

- "The Best Gift," Barbra Streisand

- "Beep, Beep," the Playmates

Horace Pippin: Inferring from the Heart

Self-taught American artist Horace Pippin painted little-noticed snippets of our daily lives, from a family meal to a game of dominoes. Pippin's unpretentious folk quality is very appealing to children. His work seems simple at first, but small clues sprinkled here and there enable us to infer and enjoy. Take *Christmas Morning, Breakfast* (1945), for example. At first kids smile at the holiday scene, noting familiar images. If given the gift of time, however, they start to make inferences.

"Look at the stocking. Since it is bulging, I'm thinking that Santa must have already come."

"The presents haven't been opened yet. I'm inferring that the mother is making the boy eat breakfast before he opens his gifts. More evidence for that is the sad expression on his face."

"Maybe this family doesn't have very much money. My evidence is the basic furniture they have, the missing plaster from the walls, and the small number of gifts under the tree."

Students can go on and on and on. They are using strategic language and seeking out evidence to support their inferences. Soon they will be asked to do these very things inside text. We can optimize their chances for success by providing plenty of opportunities for practice, with the difficulty increasing gradually over time.

Besides *Christmas Morning, Breakfast*, consider these other works of Horace Pippin for lessons around inferring: *After Supper, West Chester* (1935), *Fishing Through Ice* (1941), *The Wash* (1942), *Domino Players* (1943), and *Mr. Prejudice* (1943). Students can jot their inferences on sticky notes and place them around the edges of the print or use graphic organizers to arrange their thinking. The talk is what's most important here, though, as always! If you feel your students are ready, invite them to infer themes or big ideas from Pippin's work. When working with *Christmas Morning, Breakfast*, my students inferred big ideas like "make do with what you have" and "families have traditions."

The Wordless Books of Istvan Banyai

Almost any wordless book can be used to help students practice inferring, but Istvan Banyai's children's books are ideal. Banyai's work is like beautiful instrumental music; adding words might just ruin it! This Hungarian illustrator uses his remarkable talent to keep us guessing as we travel through his wordless wonderlands. Please note that some of Banyai's work was created for adults only, but the following titles are perfect for children: *Zoom* (1995b), *Re-Zoom* (1995a), *REM: Rapid Eye Movement* (1997), and *The Other Side* (2005; not to be confused with Jacqueline Woodson's book of the same title). Students can, of course, partner up to infer their way through these books using the thinking stems for inferring. Banyai often provides the reader with just a tiny amount of evidence to go on, fueling curiosity and encouraging inferences. What makes these books even more interesting is that students can choose to start the books at the beginning or at the end! One of my copies of

Zoom has been used so often that it has literally fallen apart at the seams. This was providential, I think, because my students started mixing the pages in random order and attempting to sequence them once again! I prompted them to use the language of inferring all along the way. No problem here. My students always want to surround Banyai's books with plenty of conversation.

Quotes About Inferring to Get Kids Talking!

Reading is important—read between the lines. Don't swallow everything.
  —*Gwendolyn Brooks, poet*

There is no surer way to misread any document than to read it literally.
  —*Learned Hand, judge*

The golden guess is morning-star to the full round of truth.
  —*Alfred Lord Tennyson, poet*

It's the stuff between the lines, the empty space between those lines which is interesting.
  —*Robert Carlyle, actor*

From a drop of water a logician could infer the possibility of an Atlantic or a Niagara without having seen or heard of one or the other.
  —*Arthur Conan Doyle, author*

Guessing what the pitcher is going to throw is eighty percent of being a successful hitter. The other twenty percent is just execution.
  —*Hank Aaron, professional baseball player*

You can't tell any kind of story without having some kind of theme, something to say between the lines.
  —*Robert Wise, filmmaker*

What I like in a good author isn't what he says, but what he whispers.
  —*Logan P. Smith, essayist*

Time for Text: Inferring

These lessons can support your students as they learn to be inferential thinkers!

Cunningham, Andie, and Ruth Shagoury. 2005. *Starting with Comprehension.* Portland, ME: Stenhouse. See Chapter 6, "Spiraling Deeper: Determining Importance and Inferring."

Harvey, Stephanie, and Anne Goudvis. 2000. *Strategies That Work.* Portland, ME: Stenhouse. See Chapter 8, "Visualizing and Inferring: Strategies That Enhance Understanding."

———. 2005. *The Comprehension Toolkit.* Portsmouth, NH: Heinemann. See Strategy Cluster Book 4, *Infer Meaning.*

Miller, Debbie. 2002. *Reading with Meaning.* Portland, ME: Stenhouse. See Chapter 8, "Inferring."

Oczkus, Lori. 2004. *Super 6 Comprehension Strategies.* Norwood, MA: Christopher-Gordon. See Chapter 4, "Inferring."

Szymusiak, Karen, and Franki Sibberson. 2001. *Beyond Leveled Books.* Portland, ME: Stenhouse. See page 18, "Inferring from the Text in a Poem," page 31, "Supporting Predictions by Finding Proof in the Book," and page 44, "Supporting Thoughts with Lines from the Text."

Tovani, Cris. 2000. *I Read It, but I Don't Get It.* Portland, ME: Stenhouse. See Chapter 8, "Outlandish Responses: Taking Inferences Too Far."

Zimmermann, Susan, and Chryse Hutchins. 2003. *7 Keys to Comprehension.* New York: Three Rivers. See Chapter 5, "Weaving Sense into Words."

Questioning
Fuel for Thought

sking questions can be downright dangerous. Damaging, even. I remember the night I learned this the hard way. It was suppertime at my granny's house, a major event indeed. Aunts, uncles, and cousins crowded into the huge country kitchen to enjoy the best food in the state of Kentucky. The men had been out fishing all day, and Granny fried up the catch. We bowed our heads as Poppy rendered thanks. As the prayer went on and on, I remember raising my four-year-old head to notice just how many people were there for dinner. Would there be enough food for everyone? More importantly, would there be enough for me? As soon as I heard the decisive amen, I called out at the top of my lungs, "Can I have a leg?" My uncles doubled over in laughter and my aunts cackled until they cried. My compassionate mother leaned in to whisper, "Sweetie, it's fish, not chicken." How could I be so stupid? I knew fish didn't have legs! I wanted to crawl under that great big table and hide. No surprise that this forty-year-old story is recounted whenever my extended family reunites. Yeah, it's *sort* of funny now, but I can still feel the stinging humiliation. I decided that very night that I would *not* ask any more questions. It was much safer just to be quiet.

And so it goes with my students. The younger they are, the more willing they seem to be publicly curious. To ask questions. To wonder. My questioning lessons are initially more successful in the primary grades than with the older kids. I understand why. They've already had "fish leg" moments. They believe that asking questions is for dummies, and they know that far too many adults don't appreciate inquisitive minds. Even worse, excessive testing has taught students to spend their energies in pursuit of the one right answer, never mind any questions that the reader might have. Neil Postman echoes this thinking when he says, "Children enter school as question marks and come out as periods" (1995, 70).

As depressing as this may seem, hope lies within the renewed emphasis on student-generated questioning! When kids learn that their own questions have value, their confidence soars, and their thinking grows exponentially. "If a child is to keep alive his inborn sense of wonder...he needs the companionship of at least one adult who can share it" (Carson 1998, 41). Rachel Carson's words remind me that I *am* that one adult to so many children. And so are you.

Michael J. Gelb's national best-seller *How to Think Like Leonardo da Vinci* (1998) contains a chapter titled "Curiosita." Before reading this, I thought I knew a lot about questioning. After all, I knew Bloom's taxonomy backward and forward and could ask high-level questions with the best of them. In spending time perfecting *my* questioning skills, however, I'd neglected developing those of my students. Michael Gelb taught me so much about the teaching of strategic questioning:

- Teach kids to ask questions. It builds upon their natural impulse for curiosity.

- Trust that the ability to ask questions can be developed.

- Remember that sometimes there's no need for answers...even in school.

- Believe that the questions we ask influence the depth of our thinking and the quality of our lives.

- Spend more time looking for the right question than the right answer.

At times I need to be prompted into a questioning state of mind. Overloaded curriculum maps and the pressures of test preparation quickly make me forget the value of wonder and curiosity. Here are some questioning quickies that can help shift the focus of your classroom.

- Hang a roll of adding machine tape in your classroom as a reminder of how questioning goes on and on and on. Encourage students to jot down anything they wonder about, without worrying about finding the answers to these questions. Soon the adding machine tape will be filled with the curiosities your students may otherwise have never revealed. What a great way to get into the minds of your kids! I always begin the roll with some of the things I often wonder about: Why do roller-coasters make me nauseated? Will the Midwest have a mild winter? How can I be a better mom to Blythe and Brynne? Should my dad get that pontoon boat? Will I ever get a dog? How many children have I taught over the course of my lifetime? Will America cease to be dependent on foreign oil? Where did I put my glasses?

- Play the "conversation of questions" game. Partners attempt to make meaningful conversation using only questions. A great example can be found in the "questions only" game on television's *Whose Line Is It Anyway?* Although this show is not suitable for elementary students, it can give you ideas for playing improvisational questioning games with your class.

- Teach your students to look for a second right answer. Don't always stop after a first right answer has been identified. Soliciting plural answers drives kids to generate deeper questions of their own.

- Instead of asking students, "What did you learn today?" try asking, "What questions did you ask today?"

No other thinking strategy has compelled me to reconsider my teaching practices more than questioning. Allowing my students to be the intensely curious beings they are has transformed me from a question-asking machine to a learning companion for my students.

Launching Sequence: Questioning

Concrete Experience: Questioning Rocks!

Materials needed: an object that holds personal significance for you, preferably one with a story behind it

My great friend and office mate Angie Ferguson travels to northern Michigan each July. As she walked the shores of Lake Huron last summer, Angie spotted a smooth, egg-shaped rock, just the shade of purple I adore. The size of my fist, Angie's rock is now part of my tried-and-true launching lesson for questioning. Kids love rocks: the weight in their hands, the unpredictable textures, the knowledge that rocks are so plentiful and accessible.

We begin in a circle. I place the rock in the palm of my hand and invite the kids to begin examining it. I don't tell them much, only that this rock is very special to me. The thinking stems for questioning are posted within sight, although many children don't seem to need them when wondering about nature. (See Figure 5–1.)

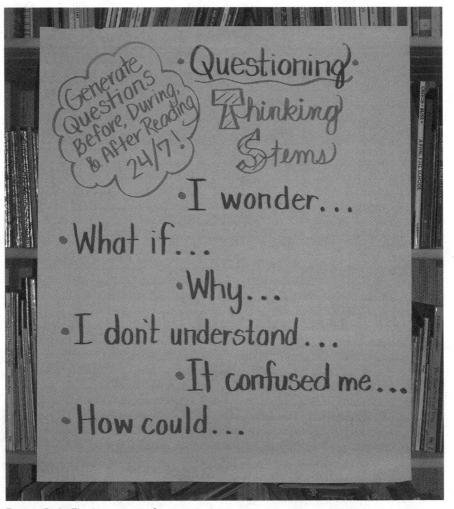

Figure 5–1 *Thinking stems for questioning*

We gently pass the rock around the circle, taking time to run our fingers around the smooth curves and notice the unexpected weight. Kids immediately fire off questions: "Where did you get this rock?" "Why is it special?" "How long have you had it?" "Is it from Ohio?" "What kind of rock is it?" "When did you first see it?" "Do you have a rock collection?" "Why does it look purple?" "How old is it?"

The questions that surface seem to sponsor new questions, until the students are satisfied that their queries have been voiced. I tell them what expert questioners they are, how their questions are even more thought provoking than the answers. I promise to provide more information about this special rock as the days go by. I compare it to reading a book; you don't get all the answers at once. The author often strings you along, and your questions fuel the drive to keep reading.

Each day I reveal a little bit more about the story of the rock, displaying it in a prominent place to spur even more questions. One group I worked with recently even placed the rock on the classroom stool, along with trailing chains of sticky notes filled with questions!

Figure 5–2 *Bobby holds the questioning rock.*

Sensory Exercises: Questioning

Q: 24/7

Each month new teacher Shannon Liechte graciously invites me into her
first-grade class at Willowville Elementary. We work with her students to
launch new thinking strategies, creating memorable anchor lessons.
Recently I related to Shannon's students how great thinkers question all the
time. The students took my language and quickly made it their own as we
turned to talk. "We should question twenty-four seven," I overheard as I listened in. I decided to follow their lead. It was no surprise that every child in
this class was familiar with the popular phrase *twenty-four seven*. One student mentioned how the neighborhood Walgreens was open twenty-four
seven. Another shared how her father was on call at the fire department
twenty-four seven. "Wow," I said. "It's like we are in the business of questioning and we're open twenty-four seven!" We decided to create a logo as
a visual prompt for this new strategy. (See Figure 5–3.)

Figure 5–3 *Our questioning logo*

I talked frankly with the students about how difficult it is to maintain a questioning stance. We talked about excessive testing and the fear of being wrong. I reminded them that we could support each other by valuing all questions posed and encouraging each other to look for more than one right answer. A few creative kids began using the American Sign Language hand gesture for *Q* whenever someone posed a particularly thoughtful question. It wasn't long before everyone caught on. Now months have passed since I launched the questioning strategy with Miss Liechte's first graders, but it's not unusual to walk down the hallway at Willowville and see a giggling child giving me the *Q* sign!

The Q Food

To get kids thinking about the practice of questioning before, during, and after reading, venture into a health food store. Pick up a bag of quinoa (pronounced "keen-wa"). Quinoa is a grain from the Andes Mountains, first used by the Incan civilization (for more information, visit www.quinoa.net). Uncommon foods are ideal for this lesson, since many students are not acquainted with the unusual names and flavors. Quinoa is inexpensive and is prepared much like rice; you'll need to cook it at home so you can quickly warm it up at school. Introduce the food by displaying it before the students and writing its name on the board. Invite students to smell and view the food up close. Chart their initial questions.

- Do I have to try it?

- Is this from another country?

- Does Mrs. McGregor like it?

- Is it expensive?

- Will I like it?

Point out to students that they haven't even tasted the food, yet they have so many questions already...just like when you pick up a book for the first time. You can have questions before ever "tasting" the words. It's these questions that make you want to open your mind and dig in!

Pass out plastic spoons and encourage your students to try the quinoa. While they savor the taste, ask the students to identify any new questions they might have. Chart them in a second column.

- Do my friends like this?

- What other foods does it taste like?

- Can I have more?

- Can I spit this out?

- Where can my parents buy this?

Talk with the students about how questions formed in their minds even as they tasted the quinoa. Again, this is just like reading a good book. Questions surface at the same time you are experiencing the text. These questions help you understand what you're reading.

Now that the students have experience with quinoa, explore what they're wondering. What fresh questions exist? What lingering questions remain?

- Does my mom know about quinoa?

- Do I have to eat any more?

- Do kids in other countries eat this all the time?

- Am I a picky eater?

- Is quinoa a healthy food?

Point out how the quinoa has been tasted and swallowed (in most cases!) and still there are questions to be asked. When a reader finishes a good book, the thinking goes on and on. Questions incubate long after the cover is closed. This savory encounter with quinoa will anchor future conversations with your students about questioning with text.

Note: Other unusual foods require less preparation and can generate the same great questions from students. My creative colleague Mary Taylor suggests using any or all of the following: daikon radishes, prickly pear cactus fruit, Ugli fruit, star fruit, purple kale, kumquat.

Wonder-full Songs

Songwriters often fill their lyrics with questions. It's great for kids to hear the power of questions within the context of music. As always, provide students with a copy of the lyrics. Ask them to notice how the questions are used, how the questions change their thinking, and if the lyrics give answers to the questions posed. These songs ask the listener one question after another:

- "Whose Garden Was This," Tom Paxton

- "Blowin' in the Wind," Bob Dylan

- "Y," by Mark McGuinn

Other songs might not use questions in their lyrics, but they surely generate questions in the mind of the listener. Students become fluent questioners as they listen and wonder. These titles have worked for me:

- "Eleanor Rigby," the Beatles

- "The Living Years," Mike and the Mechanics

Vermeer: Questions Beneath the Surface

The life of Jan Vermeer (1632–75) is shrouded in the unknown. Although much has been written about his modest life and sizeable family, most of what is known is based in supposition. Since no writings or letters by the artist have been found to date, not even any sales records from his lifetime, we can only guess about his artistic influences and personality. The little we do know makes us hunger for more. Novels like *Girl with a Pearl Earring*, by Tracy Chevalier (2001), *Girl in Hyacinth Blue*, by Susan Vreeland (2000), and *Chasing Vermeer*, by Blue Balliett (2005) attempt to satisfy us with inferred scenarios and creative speculation.

The same is true of Vermeer's work. The situations depicted are ambiguous; the painted figures seem lost in furtive thought. At first the viewer might appreciate the beauty and tranquility of the paintings, but questions lurk just beneath the surface. Who were Vermeer's subjects? What were they thinking? Did we catch them by surprise? That our questions can never be answered only makes them more provoking…an ideal place to lead our students as they consider the power of questioning.

Build children's schema by providing some background information about Vermeer. Tell them of his wife and eleven children, the family's inn, and the rediscovery of his work two centuries after it was painted. Introduce students to the obscurity shrouding his work, and allow them to spend time studying some of his paintings. The questions are sure to come: dozens of theirs and a few of yours, too.

Kids seem to be especially interested in *A Girl Asleep* (c. 1657), *Girl Reading a Letter at an Open Window* (c. 1657), *The Girl with the Pearl Earring* (c. 1665), and *The Love Letter* (c. 1669–70).

The Wordless Books of David Wiesner

Nothing fills children with wonder more than gazing into the sky. Is a storm approaching? Where will that jet land? Could that be the Little Dipper? Doesn't that cloud look like a dinosaur? Author-illustrator David Wiesner capitalizes on this inborn curiosity in three of his wordless books: *Free Fall* (1988), *Tuesday* (1991), and *Sector 7* (1999). In these inventive books, the sky is the setting for fantastic adventures and unending questions. Try a before, during, and after questioning session with your students.

Before: Have students ask questions while examining the front and back covers, the dedication, the blurb, and the biographical information.

During: Develop questioning fluency in students by encouraging them to ask their questions aloud during the viewing of the book. I do this without requiring students to raise their hands. When a question arises, the student simply asks it aloud. Kids are bursting in and out with their questions, popcorn style. Another option is to challenge kids to investigate these books with a friend, using only questions as conversation.

After: Have students go eye-to-eye with a partner and contemplate the following: What are you wondering? What doesn't make sense? Which part of the story raised the most questions for you? How did your questions propel you through the book? Are you left with unanswered questions?

With Wiesner's wordless books, the sky's the limit for questioning!

Quotes About Questioning to Get Kids Talking!

One's first step in wisdom is to question everything.
   —*Georg Christoph Lichtenberg, scientist*

The important thing is not to stop questioning.
   —*Albert Einstein, physicist*

The answers aren't important really.... What's important is—knowing all the questions.
   —*Zilpha Keatley Snyder, author*

It is better to know some of the questions than all of the answers.
   —*James Thurber, humorist*

Not to know is bad; not to wish to know is worse.
   —*African proverb*

Judge of a man by his questions rather than by his answers.
   —*Voltaire, philosopher*

All men by nature desire to know.
   —*Aristotle, philosopher*

The desire to know is natural to good men.
   —*Leonardo Da Vinci, artist*

Time for Text: Questioning

No more wondering where to find great questioning lessons. Check out these ideas!

Cunningham, Andie, and Ruth Shagoury. 2005. *Starting with Comprehension*. Portland, ME: Stenhouse. See Chapter 5, "Asking Questions Together."

Harvey, Stephanie, and Anne Goudvis. 2000. *Strategies That Work*. Portland, ME: Stenhouse. See Chapter 7, "Questioning: The Strategy That Propels Readers Forward."

———. 2005. *The Comprehension Toolkit*. Portsmouth, NH: Heinemann. See Strategy Cluster Book 3, *Ask Questions*.

Hoyt, Linda. 2000. *Snapshots*. Portsmouth, NH: Heinemann. See page 16, "'I Wonder' Questions," and page 144, "Question It."

———. 2002. *Make It Real*. Portsmouth, NH: Heinemann. See Chapter 10, "Taking the Time to Wonder: Questioning Strategies to Build Comprehension" and page 192, "Questioning as You Go."

Miller, Debbie. 2002. *Reading with Meaning*. Portland, ME: Stenhouse. See Chapter 9, "Asking Questions."

Oczkus, Lori. 2004. *Super 6 Comprehension Strategies*. Norwood, MA: Christopher-Gordon. See Chapter 5, "Questioning."

Tovani, Cris. 2000. *I Read It, but I Don't Get It*. Portland, ME: Stenhouse. See Chapter 7, "What Do You Wonder?"

Zimmermann, Susan, and Chryse Hutchins. 2003. *7 Keys to Comprehension*. New York: Three Rivers. See Chapter 4, "Why, What, Where, Who, and How."

Determining Importance

Under the Big Top

A visit to the circus is an exercise in determining importance. I should know. Going to the circus is an annual event for the McGregor family. Every spring the television commercials transmit their alluring calls to my daughters, Blythe and Brynne. Every spring my husband, Miles, and I decide we just won't go this year. Every year we do. And why wouldn't we want to go? Where else can we be surrounded by hoards of overstimulated kids begging for cotton candy and high-priced plastic toys? Where else can we bombard our brains with gratuitous sound, color, smell, and action for two eternal hours?

When Blythe was little, maybe four or five years old, she was puzzled by the whole circus experience. I remember settling into our crowded seats, only to hear her tiny voice say, "Mommy, what am I supposed to look at first?" A difficult question to answer, for sure. In addition to the three rings filled with acrobats, elephants, and daredevils, there were juggling clowns and sparkly dancers vying for our attention, not to mention the reverberating voice of the emcee, the annoying shouts of the food vendors, and the amplified circus band. Blythe's question prompted me to think about determining importance. Our children need to know how to single out and process what is meaningful, and how to recognize and set aside the distracters, in text and in daily life. I see this strategy as essential, now more than ever. Kids face the determining-importance dilemma everywhere they turn. In *7 Keys to Comprehension,* Zimmermann and Hutchins (2003) cite CNN as another example of how we are inundated with information. With pencil and paper in hand, I recently decided to experience this barrage myself, taking note of how many kinds of text and images were presented in only five minutes. It's just like going to the circus! I saw graphs, maps, titles, subheadings, bulleted information, the figures from the Dow, NASDAQ, and S&P, pictures within pictures, scrolling weather and news, three changes of anchors and sets, the time in three zones, plus the correspondents' names and credits. And don't forget the short, intense bursts of music and dramatic commentary! Granted, our students are growing up in an age of information, and some say they can process stimuli more effectively than adults can. Unfortunately, my colleagues and I do not see this skill transfer into strategic reading. Some kids even seem to rely on flashy, fast-paced presentation, which makes connecting to unadorned text seem dull. We've learned not to assume that our students know how to filter out the fluff and focus on the facts. What is needed now is thoughtful conversation and explicit teaching around the strategy of determining importance. Kids need all the support we can give as they navigate their way through this technology-driven age of information.

In this chapter, I approach determining importance in a personal way. Many of the examples and quotations have to do with determining what's important in one's everyday life. It has been my experience that this approach quickly draws kids into the conversation and helps them see this strategy as relevant. When kids start thinking and talking about what's important to them, about how they determine what matters most, they are better able to detect and discuss what's essential in text when the time comes.

Everyday conversations with your students can help introduce the language of determining importance and serve as a transition into strategy instruction. Start by posting the thinking stems for determining importance. (See Figure 6–1.)

Prompt your students to use the stems as they answer questions like these:

- Think of all of the things you did today. What was the most important?

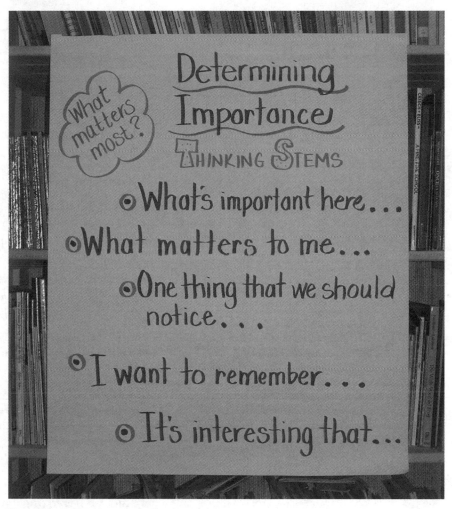

Figure 6–1 *Thinking stems for determining importance*

- What is one thing that you want to remember about today's lesson [or story or discussion]?

- What is the most important thing you learned today?

Be sure to ask the students to provide a rationale for their answers. By inviting kids to be metacognitive about these responses, we show that we value the process, not just the product, of determining importance.

Launching Sequence: Determining Importance

Concrete Experience: Purses

Materials needed: your purse, backpack, briefcase, or school bag, filled with selected items for kids to discuss

It's a fact: Kids are intensely curious about their teachers' personal lives and belongings. They want to know what kind of car we drive and how we spend our weekends. To know us as human beings is to make meaning of us. I remember when my own third-grade teacher, Mrs. Turner, left her purse in the copy room and sent me to retrieve it. Since it was slightly unzipped, I had *no choice* but to peek inside. Wrigley's Spearmint gum! Cool! My teacher chewed gum—the very thing she made her students avoid. (No, I didn't ever share this classified information with my friends; I kept it a secret until now.) I remember feeling like it was my lucky day; I knew a little something about Mrs. Turner that was discovered quite by accident. This small memory was the seed for the following lesson idea. I decided to tap the natural curiosity that students have about their teachers and channel it into a conversation about determining importance.

Most recently I taught this lesson with Donna King's fifth-grade class at Brantner Elementary. Donna knew her students were struggling with determining importance, so we decided to start at the very beginning with something concrete. Without introduction, I started class with my purse on my lap. (If you don't carry a purse, no problem. A school bag, briefcase, or backpack will do just fine.) I explained that I was going to the walking track after school and didn't want to carry my purse along with me. It would be easier to take only what was really important. I invited the students to look at the contents of my purse (selected with this lesson in mind, of course) to help me decide what was important to take along as I exercised and what could remain in my purse. I arranged my belongings in plain view: my driver's license, my cell phone, a pack of gum, keys, my inhaler, a tube of lipstick, and an Old Navy coupon. (See Figure 6–2.)

Figure 6–2 *The contents of Mrs. McGregor's purse*

After identifying each object, I asked the students to turn and talk as I listened in. It made me smile when I heard how seriously they considered each item! Students were using the language of determining importance, and I jotted down pieces of their conversations in my notebook.

■ If you have asthma like Mrs. McGregor, it's important to have your inhaler with you at all times. She'd better take that along.

▨ Some of her stuff is just extra. She won't need it while she's taking a walk. Like the gum. It's not that important. Hopefully she can live without a pack of gum while she takes a walk!

▨ It's like you could put those things in order from really important to not very important.

▨ She only needs her keys and her cell phone. The rest of it is important sometimes, but not for going to the track.

▨ Knowing Mrs. McGregor, she will think her lipstick is important. It isn't, though...but it all depends on who is deciding what matters and what doesn't.

The thinking of these students guided the teaching that followed. As I pulled the class back together, I praised the kids for employing a strategy that proficient readers use: determining importance. I explained how using this thinking strategy can make even complicated text easier to get through.

Sensory Exercises: Determining Importance

Just Add Water!

Tina Reno's students at Withamsville-Tobasco Elementary are an amazing group to work with. Tina's high expectations and focused strategy work yield huge dividends; I know I'm in for a treat when I walk into room 124. When Tina decided to begin determining importance with her class, we started planning with the end in mind. What was it we wanted them to know? To be able to do? We settled on this: Kids should know that all words, sentences, or paragraphs are not created equal. Some carry more weight than others. These students could begin to separate the fact from the fluff.

A simple exercise helped Tina's students remember what the process of determining importance is all about. We brought in two cooking pots, a large plastic strainer, and a bag of partially cooked spaghetti. As the children gathered around, we placed the spaghetti into one of the pots and filled it with water. "Have you ever noticed how difficult it is to remember every-thing you read?" I asked. "Our brains just can't seem to hold all of that information at the same time. But that's OK! Thoughtful readers use a spe-cial strategy to deal with this problem; it's called determining importance. Mrs. Reno and I are going to help you learn how to pick out the important stuff and cast aside the minor details. This demonstration is a model of what a reader's brain does when it is reading. Watch what happens. Think about how two pans, a strainer, and some spaghetti can represent determining importance when you read." You would've thought we were performing magic or something. Every eye was wide. Just add water to any teaching moment and you'll instantly elevate the attention level.

I placed the strainer onto the empty pot and then picked up the pot con-taining the pasta and water. Ever so slowly, I poured the contents through the strainer. I lifted the dripping strainer out of the pan so everyone could see. Now I know many of these kids had witnessed the straining of pasta before, but you'd have never known it by the looks on their faces. "This lit-tle experiment is not just about spaghetti and water. It is about our brains when we read, how we try to determine what is important and remember it. Now turn and talk to your partner. Make sense of what you've just seen. How is good reading like preparing spaghetti?" The classroom buzzed with ideas, so I captured some of them in my notebook.

- Your brain is like the strainer and the words are like the noodles.

- The spaghetti water is not important so you don't have to keep it.

- You want to keep only the good stuff in your brain when you read.

- When you read something it's like it's pouring in through your eyes and then it goes through your brain.

- Is this why my mom calls my head my noodle?

Another high-interest experience that can reinforce determining impor-tance is using a flashlight in a darkened room. (See Figure 6–3.) Place large photos, illustrations, or text on an easel and then model determining impor-tance by spotlighting words or details of significance. Invite students to fol-low your lead, shining the flashlight on what is important to them. Ask each volunteer to give thinking to support his decisions.

PHOTOGRAPH BY SUSAN HEINZE

Figure 6–3 *Highlighting text in Shannon's classroom*

Listening for Importance

Don't forget to check out your own music collection, looking for song lyrics that carry a strong theme or talk about what is important. When using a song for this purpose, don't hesitate to play it more than once. We all know the benefits of rereading, and it's the same with relistening! Play the song once for pure enjoyment. The second time, ask students to begin to listen for important ideas, often signaled by repetition. Some kids might even jot down powerful words or lines. After the second listen, invite kids to turn and talk about what seems important. When students have heard the thinking of a classmate, play the song once more, allowing the listeners to fine-tune (no pun intended) their thinking. Great conversation is generated after an experience with a meaningful song. One of my favorites is "Coat of Many Colors," by Dolly Parton, which is also available as a picture book of the same title (1994). In Teresa Hennessey's third-grade class at Amelia Elementary, the students determined three important lines from Parton's autobiographical picture book.

- "made only from rags but I wore it so proudly"

- "although we had no money I was rich as I could be"

- "one is only poor only if they choose to be"

Teresa's students were able to articulate why these lines were more significant than others, why these phrases carried the message of the song. Teresa and I felt confident that these students demonstrated deep listening comprehension. They were able, through conversation, to filter through the lyric set and identify the valuable ideas, a true demonstration of determining importance. Take a listen to the following songs, too, which support conversation and thinking about determining importance:

- "Seasons of Love," from *Rent*

- "Takes a Little Time," Amy Grant

- "Secret o' Life," James Taylor

- "Ebony and Ivory," Paul McCartney and Stevie Wonder

- "Black and White," Three Dog Night

Cassatt: Make an Impression with Determining Importance

The life of American Impressionist painter Mary Cassatt (1844–1926) is a lesson in determining importance and how what's deemed important can change over time. At the early age of fifteen, Cassatt decided that becoming a great artist was all that mattered. One year later she enrolled in a prestigious art school, although it was unusual for a female to pursue a career in art. After moving to Paris in the 1860s, Cassatt overcame one prejudice after another, enjoying early success before 1870. The rest is truly history! Cassatt's images of mothers, teacups, and children are everywhere, from museums and galleries to bookstores and card shops. The accessibility of her prints can make your lesson planning a breeze.

For young learners, consider relating Cassatt's story of resolve against the discrimination of society—how she determined what was important in her life and worked to develop her talents. Primary students will be especially interested in Cassatt's later work, from around 1890 and beyond, where children are the central figures. Invite students to determine what is important in each print. They'll be sure to notice the repeating themes of childhood, motherhood, and love. My favorites are *The Child's Bath* (1893), *Breakfast in Bed* (1897), and *Young Mother* (1900).

The evolution of Cassatt's work is a fascinating illustration of determining importance for students who are ready to appreciate irony. What Mary Cassatt deemed important changed over the course of her lifetime. Show kids some Cassatt paintings from the early years, say, the late 1860s through 1880, like *At the Opera* (1877–78), *Woman in a Loge* (1878–79), and *Tea* (1879). Your local library will likely house biographies containing these and other reproductions. Most of these works feature adult women without children. No coincidence, since during this time Mary was focused solely on herself and her career. What was important to Mary surfaced in her work. By way of contrast, introduce students to Cassatt's later, more famous paintings that highlight the relationship between mother and child. This change in focus represents a change in what was important to Mary. How ironic that Mary never had children of her own, yet critics think that painting mothers and children was a way of experiencing motherhood. After providing this background knowledge, support students as they distinguish between Cassatt's early and later paintings, and facilitate discussion about how what is important to a person makes all the difference in her life's work.

Wordless Book: *A Circle of Friends*

Portfolios.com provides a fitting appraisal: Giora Carmi's award-winning work is "good for children and smart people." Carmi's illustrations have appeared in the *Wall Street Journal* and the *New York Times*. He has illustrated more than forty children's books and over two hundred book covers. Carmi's wordless book, *A Circle of Friends* (2003), is picture perfect for determining importance, with its powerful story and simple, clean drawings. Carmi uses ink lines with only one person or object per page in full color, making this book easy to use with a large group.

The book has a pay-it-forward theme, and what is important on each page jumps out at the reader, focusing on what will carry the kindness ahead. Whether you are working with young learners or with adults, just immerse them in *A Circle of Friends* with lots of talk, and the important ideas will easily surface.

Wordless books are a great fit for the teaching of determining importance. Using highlighting tape or sticky tabs, have partners explore a wordless book, identifying what is important. If each student has a different-color tape or tab, each can feel free to make personal decisions about what's important and also easily see when his conclusions coincide with those of his partner. In addition, this process works well with calendar pictures, art reproductions, and big books.

Quotes About Determining Importance to Get Kids Talking!

The truth is more important than the facts.
  —*Frank Lloyd Wright, architect*

In your thirst for knowledge, be sure not to drown in all the information.
  —*Anthony J. D'Angelo, author*

The most important thing in life is to learn how to give out love, and to let it come in.
  —*Morrie Schwartz, educator*

From the time we're born until we die, we're kept busy with artificial stuff that isn't important.
  —*Tom Ford, fashion designer*

The most important things to do in the world are to get something to eat, something to drink, and somebody to love you.

—*Brenda Ueland, writer*

Imagination is more important than knowledge.

—*Albert Einstein, physicist*

Remember then that there is only one important time, and that time is now.

—*Jon J. Muth, author*

Most of the important things in the world have been accomplished by people who have kept on trying when there seemed to be no hope at all.

—*Dale Carnegie, writer*

Time for Text: Determining Importance

Move ahead with lessons specifically designed to empower your students as they mine the text for what's important.

Cunningham, Andie, and Ruth Shagoury. 2005. *Starting with Comprehension*. Portland, ME: Stenhouse. See Chapter 6, "Spiraling Deeper: Determining Importance and Inferring."

Harvey, Stephanie, and Anne Goudvis. 2000. *Strategies That Work*. Portland, ME: Stenhouse. See Chapter 9, "Determining Importance in Text: The Nonfiction Connection."

———. 2005. *The Comprehension Toolkit*. Portsmouth, NH: Heinemann. See Strategy Cluster Book 5, *Determine Importance*.

Hoyt, Linda. 2000. *Snapshots*. Portsmouth, NH: Heinemann. See page 181, "Key Words to Summarize."

————. 2002. *Make It Real*. Portsmouth, NH: Heinemann. See page 189, "Very Important Points Strategy (VIP)," and page 201, "Rank Ordering Information."

Miller, Debbie. 2002. *Reading with Meaning*. Portland, ME: Stenhouse. See Chapter 10, "Determining Importance in Nonfiction."

Oczkus, Lori. 2004. *Super 6 Comprehension Strategies*. Norwood, MA: Christopher-Gordon. See Chapter 8, "Evaluating."

Zimmermann, Susan, and Chryse Hutchins. 2003. *7 Keys to Comprehension*. New York: Three Rivers. See Chapter 6, "What's Important and Why."

Visualizing

See for Yourself

icture this: Saturday morning, eight o'clock. One sleepy dad baking cinnamon rolls, two bed-headed daughters sitting at the kitchen table, and one mom who is thinking about a new chapter.

MOM: Do you like it when movies are made from books you've read?

BLYTHE (*age 10*): I loved watching *The Chronicles of Narnia* because it matched the pictures I had in my head from reading the book. I would see something and think, "Yes. That's what I saw when I read."

BRYNNE (*age 9*): Well, that's not what happened with *Charlie and the Chocolate Factory*! I felt confused when I watched the original version of the movie. But it ended up being a good thing because it made me keep comparing the book and the movie all the way through. It was like a Venn diagram in my head.

BLYTHE: I like reading the book first so I can make the pictures before I see them. But I saw *Harry Potter and the Sorcerer's Stone* before I read the book, and then when I did read it, my pictures matched the movie. This can be good or bad. It can help you to have pictures already in your mind, but it can also take away pictures you invent.

DAD: I've got to say it bothered me when I heard that Tom Hanks would be the lead in the movie of *The da Vinci Code*. Not that I don't like his acting, but the whole time I was reading the book I had already cast Harrison Ford to play the lead role.

BRYNNE: I don't like pictures to get in my head before I read the book. If you see the movie first, it's like your own ideas get erased out of your head forever.

MOM: Do you ever have trouble visualizing while you're reading? What do you do?

BLYTHE: Sometimes I need help getting the pictures. Like with the Beacon Street Girls series, I started with book five and I couldn't get the background in my mind from the other books, so I went to the Internet. Some books have Internet sites where you can see pictures that might help you understand the book. That is an easy way to get images if you are having trouble.

DAD: If I get distracted or lose the pictures in my head, I reread to try to start them up again. I also know to slow my reading pace, and usually that helps.

BRYNNE: I like drawing what I see. It helps me because when you do it in your mind, you think you have all the information you can think of. But when you draw it, all of the details come out on the paper, and you didn't even realize they were there.

BLYTHE: Drawing mental images is not helpful to me because my mind can draw better than my hand can. The artwork in my head is like what a famous artist could paint. But I can't draw like that yet. If my teacher asks me to draw my mental images, I feel frustrated because it doesn't turn out like what I imagined. I would way rather talk about it than draw it. I can explain what I was seeing and I feel better about that.

This breakfast conversation reminds me of several things. One, I've been talking about thinking strategies *way* too much around my family. My husband and kids sound just like reading teachers! Two, the process and product of one's visualization are so personal. While each person's images are unique and valuable, not everyone feels comfortable sharing his mental pictures through drawing. Three, our engagement with information, be it through books or media, is deepened through the creation of images in our minds.

Jeffrey Wilhelm goes as far as to say that "without visualization, students cannot comprehend, and reading cannot be said to be reading" (2004, 9).

Writers themselves can provide exceptional insight into this strategy. A wonderful little book titled *Madeleine L'Engle Herself* (2001) taught me so much about the convergence of reading, writing, and thinking. L'Engle gives special consideration to the power of visualization. "Reading is an incredibly creative act. Once a schoolchild asked about all of the illustrations in my books and was a little bit surprised that they're not illustrated. He'd read them and seen the illustrations in his own mind. So to read a book is to create a book. To read a book is to listen, to visualize, to see. If the reader, child or adult, cannot create the book along with the writer, the book is stillborn" (164).

Since our students are absolutely accustomed to visual literacies— websites, cartoons, movies, print media, and so on—how smart we would be to regard this as a teaching and learning advantage! By appreciating our students' affinity for the visual, and by noticing and naming visualization as a thinking strategy, we can bolster motivation and confidence as our kids become stronger readers.

Launching Sequence: Visualizing

Concrete Experience: A Room with a View

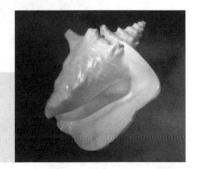

Materials needed: one cardboard tube for each student (the tube from a roll of paper towels can be cut into thirds), objects from nature, drawing paper

Kids always like to be around when it's time to wrap gifts. It's not so much that they enjoy the act of giving...it has more to do with playing with the cardboard tubes when the wrapping paper is gone! Whenever I use cardboard tubes at school, most kids are inclined to use them as a spyglass. When we use a viewfinder, the world changes. Objects become clearer, colors more vivid. Cardboard tubes are ideal to use for the introduction of visualizing...and it's easy to amass a collection of these tools to help launch the study of visualizing. All you need is a cardboard tube for each student; the ones from toilet paper rolls and paper towels work perfectly.

The second graders in Vikki Henshey's class were just as I expected: eager to get their hands on the cardboard tubes and spy around the classroom. At first I let the kids experiment, looking out the window, at each other, and around the room.

After a few minutes, I got them settled back into their seats. I asked them to turn and talk about why it seems so interesting to look through these tubes.

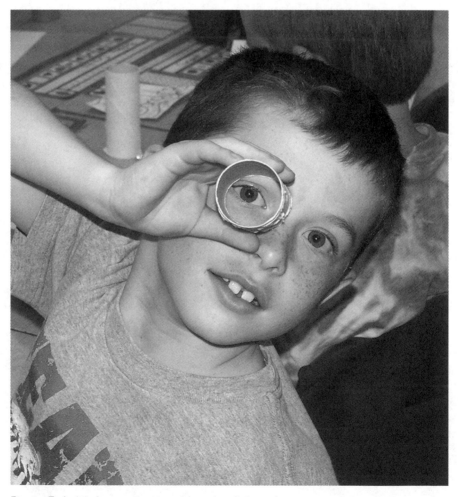

Figure 7–1 *Jacob experiments with a visualizing tube*

- The world looks different.

- It is like I am in another room looking through a keyhole.

- It looks cool because the tube makes it dark all around the thing you are looking at.

- I can focus better.

Next I asked the students to use their visualizing tubes (as they've come to be called) to focus on one of the concrete items I had positioned around the classroom. Perched on top of file cabinets, bookshelves, and tables were placed a variety of items: a conch shell, a large pinecone, a potted plant, a rusty metal bucket, a small bird feeder. I invited the kids to spend a couple of minutes looking through the tubes at the items. I asked them to choose one item that captured their interest, maybe something that triggered a memory or seemed particularly interesting. Kids spent time looking at the chosen object, picturing where it might belong (in the forest? on a back porch?) and visualizing what sights, smells, sounds, and sensations might be surrounding it. Then the students sketched their visualizations on plain paper or found a friend to talk with about their mental images. After kids had a chance to think deeply about their images, I grouped students according to the objects they had chosen. This gave kids the chance to notice how everyone sees things in different ways, how our visualizations are as individual as we are.

I then explained to the class how this experience connects with reading. "Sometimes when you read, the writing helps you focus on something. Your brain can see it clearly, as if you were right there. Not only can you see with your mind, but sometimes you can smell, taste, hear, and feel as well. We can call this visualizing, or making mental or sensory images. We have the ability to create these sensations in our heads, just by reading the print on the page. It's like magic! Being able to visualize makes reading so much more fun. Turn and talk to a friend about a time when you read something or someone read to you and you could actually see or feel what was going on in the text." As usual, the kids had lots of great examples.

- When my mom read *Mrs. Piggle-Wiggle* to my brother and me, I closed my eyes and could still see what was going on.

- Mrs. Henshey reads out loud to us and I can picture what's happening because she uses different voices.

■ When I read *Toes*, I could see all the crazy things the cat did. I was picturing my own cat in my mind when I read that book.

■ It sort of feels like dreams in my head when I read something really good.

This concrete experience creates a wonderful opportunity to launch conversation about visualization, to emphasize our interesting differences, and to allow kids to indulge in a simple childhood pleasure: looking through a cardboard tube!

Sensory Exercises: Visualizing

Time-Tested and Teacher Approved

There are many easy ways to reinforce the practice of creating visual images, and many of these ideas have been used for decades. When framed with conversation filled with strategic language, however, these exercises turn from superficial to substantive. As kids begin to talk about this strategy, encourage them to refer to the thinking stems chart. (See Figure 7–2.)

Consider the following list of sensory supports:

■ Have students listen to an old radio show with a partner (check your public library). They can pause every five to seven minutes to turn and talk about what images they've created.

■ Have students listen to a read-aloud while drawing in sketchbooks.

■ Soak cotton balls in familiar liquids (orange juice, mouthwash, salad dressing, suntan oil, etc.). Place the cotton balls in small plastic bags. Circulate the bags and discuss the mental images that are fostered by the smells.

■ Pass around paper bags with mystery objects inside. As students handle each object, they can talk to a partner about what they "see."

■ Have students search magazines for images that support a certain topic or theme.

■ Ask students to create a time line using only pictures.

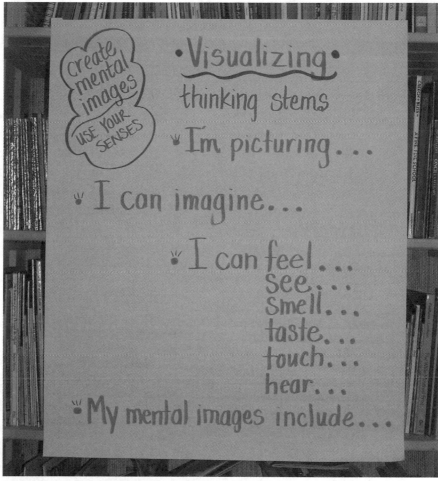

Figure 7–2 *Thinking stems for visualizing*

<ul>
<li>Have children listen to a picture book without looking at the illustrations. Then they can reread it themselves and notice how their mental images change as they assimilate the images of the illustrator.</li>

<li>Have kids listen to a recording of everyday sounds. They can talk about the images that they conjure up as they listen.</li>

<li>Have students look at a book of optical illusions. This is a wonderful way to begin conversations about how your brain sees in a different way than your eyes do.</li>
</ul>

Mental Images Through Music

Music is precisely the vehicle through which kids can learn to visualize. Songs speak directly to our brains, evoking highly sensory mental images and pairing them with emotion. Songwriters use imagery more than any other device, enabling the listener to develop the ability to visualize.

Some students know how to sit back and enjoy listening to music; often these children experience rich mental images while appreciating songs. Many more students, however, lack a musical schema, not having been exposed to much more than their parents' favorite radio station. Capturing time to relax, listen, and imagine with music can support the beginnings of visual creativity for many children. With so many of my students, the music we share gives them their very first experiences with mental imagery. Be on the lookout for music that gives kids the freedom to create. Here are a few pieces that my students have enjoyed:

- "Old Friends/Bookends," Simon and Garfunkel

- "English Tea," Paul McCartney

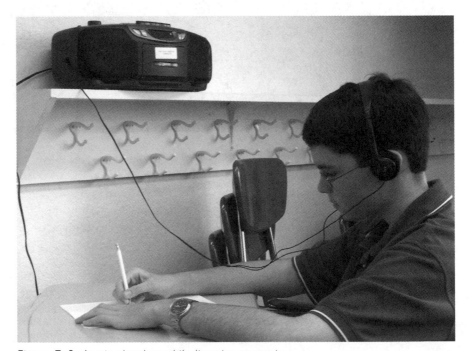

Figure 7–3 *Austin sketches while listening to music.*

- "The Marvelous Toy," Tom Paxton

- "Grandma's Feather Bed," John Denver

In many cases, I find that song lyrics support my students as they create mental images. Some students find initial success, however, with instrumental pieces. Here are a few suggestions for instrumental pieces; your music teacher can suggest many more.

- *Fantasia* soundtrack

- *Pictures at an Exhibition,* Modest Mussorgsky

- *Peter and the Wolf,* Sergei Prokofiev

- *1812 Overture,* Pyotr Tchaikovsky

- *Nutcracker Suite,* Pyotr Tchaikovsky

- *Hoe Down* from *Rodeo,* Aaron Copland

Dorothea Lange: True Vision

It only makes sense that if we want to learn how to see, to teach our students to see, we should spend time with a master. Spend some time with Dorothea Lange and you'll understand. Every time I experience her wondrous photographs, I redefine what it means to visualize. I look at Lange's work and realize that seeing is not about colors, and not even so much about the subjects. Seeing is about feeling. It's about how your senses reassign your emotions and thoughts. Learning about Lange's life and art can provide a way to help students practice visualizing settings, people, and even ideas.

Kids are more interested in Lange's work when they catch a glimpse of her childhood and learn how personal tragedy only served as motivation. Dorothea was stricken with polio when she was only seven, and she was nicknamed Limpy by the neighborhood children. Her father left the family when Dorothea was twelve, never to return. Dorothea grew up feeling invisible and disconnected. That is, until she attached herself, both literally and figuratively, to a camera. Before she even owned a camera, Dorothea decided that being a photographer was what she should do with her life. Dorothea eventually traveled America, then the world, capturing the sights, smells, and sounds of the human condition in her photographs. She went on to become internationally known, teaching us to see ourselves in a more honest way. Lange held the gift of "thereness," just the characteristic we wish for our readers. She experienced each moment in a sensory dimension, her mind open to every new thought and experience.

Let your students spend time with Dorothea. Share her story and photographs, all the while noticing the sensory images they evoke. Use prompts like these as you talk about what these pictures help you see.

- What lies just beyond the frame of the photo?
- What sounds would surround this moment in time?
- How would the air feel? Dry? Humid? Still?
- Can you smell anything in this photo?
- What feelings rise up in you?

As always, the schema your students bring to the table will directly impact their responses. Expect and appreciate this beautiful diversity!

Collections of Dorothea Lange's work are available in bookstores and online. Some of her more famous works are ideal for evoking sensory images. Look for "Migrant Mother" (1936), "Alabama Farm" (1938), "Homeless Family" (1938), "Riverbank Gas Station" (1940), "New York City" (1952), and "Jake Jones's Hands" (1953).

Wordless Book: *Sidewalk Circus*

Sometimes only a child can truly *see*. In *Sidewalk Circus*, two young children are able to *see* the circus before it even comes to town. Paul Fleischman and Kevin Hawkes (2004) unite to give us this brilliant wordless book, perfect for pointing out the imaginative power of children. After conceiving this story, Fleischman recognized that his ideas would best be communicated without words. Hawkes' vibrant illustrations lead us down the city sidewalk, looking through the eyes of a child. As always, surround this wordless book with lots of opportunities for student-to-student talk. Students will merge inferring and visualization to bolster their conversation around the experience of *Sidewalk Circus*.

Other wordless series easily support visualization. Acquaint your students with the many wordless books of Emily Arnold McCully and the Carl the Dog series by Alexandra Day. Students will create mental pictures beyond the illustrations on the pages, constructing meaning with each pleasurable step.

Quotes About Visualizing to Get Kids Talking!

When your head's full of pictures, they have to come out.
> —*Bill Maynard, author*

The true seeing is within.
> —*George Eliot, novelist*

I visualize things in my mind before I have to do them. It's like having a mental workshop.
> —*Jack Youngblood, professional football player*

Imagination is the true magic carpet.
> —*Norman Vincent Peale, theologian*

The man who has no imagination has no wings.
> —*Muhammad Ali, professional boxer*

A good snapshot stops a moment from running away.
> —*Eudora Welty, writer*

All thought depends upon the image.
> —*Ferdinand de Saussure, linguist*

Words serve as fixatives for mental images.
> —*Selma H. Frailberg, medical researcher*

Time for Text: Visualizing

Need ideas for great text and thoughtful lessons with a focus on visualizing? Here are some resources to see you on your way!

Cunningham, Andie, and Ruth Shagoury. 2005. *Starting with Comprehension*. Portland, ME: Stenhouse. See Chapter 4, "Using Movement, Mind Pictures, and Metaphor to Comprehend."

Harvey, Stephanie, and Anne Goudvis. 2000. *Strategies That Work*. Portland, ME: Stenhouse. See Chapter 8, "Visualizing and Inferring: Strategies That Enhance Understanding."

Hoyt, Linda. 2000. *Snapshots*. Portsmouth, NH: Heinemann. See pages 43–46, "Visualizing During Reading."

———. **2002.** *Make It Real*. Portsmouth, NH: Heinemann. See Chapter 11, "Love Those Visuals: Photographs, Diagrams, and Learning to Love Captions."

Miller, Debbie. 2002. *Reading with Meaning*. Portland, ME: Stenhouse. See Chapter 6, "Creating Mental Images."

Oczkus, Lori. 2004. *Super 6 Comprehension Strategies*. Norwood, MA: Christopher-Gordon. See the section titled, "Can You See It?"

Szymusiak, Karen, and Franki Sibberson. 2001. *Beyond Leveled Books*. Portland, ME: Stenhouse. See page 33, "Reading Descriptive Language to Visualize Settings."

Tovani, Cris. 2000. *I Read It, but I Don't Get It*. Portland, ME: Stenhouse. See Chapter 5, "Fix It!" and Appendix C.

Wilhelm, Jeffrey D. 2004. *Reading IS Seeing*. New York: Scholastic.

Zimmermann, Susan, and Chryse Hutchins. 2003. *7 Keys to Comprehension*. New York: Three Rivers. See Chapter 2, "Motion Picture of the Mind."

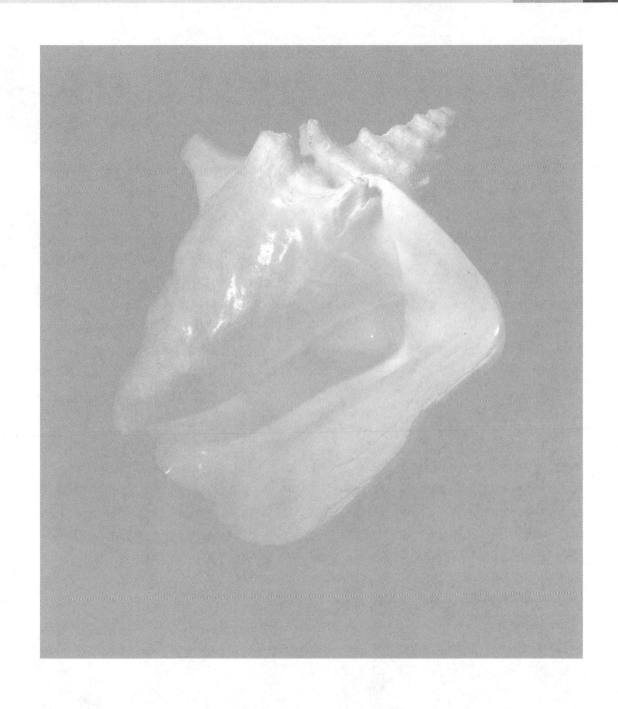

Synthesizing

Keep the Change

childhood visit to my aunt Freda's house was always a treat. I would spend time exploring her basement, which was full of old books and records, and then come upstairs for the sweetest pineapple upside-down cake the world has ever tasted. No visit to Aunt Freda's was complete, however, without playing with the wooden nesting dolls. I would sit on the scalloped carpet, taking the dolls apart one by one and then reassembling them in a disciplined way. I remember thinking how all the dolls were important. The smallest one established the form for all the rest, yet the largest one safely encapsulated all of the others. If one doll was missing, the progression would be incomplete.

What a beautiful model of synthesizing! As we read, original thought takes shape, and then it expands as we encounter new information. All the while, the new and the old are in relationship with each other, a natural evolution of thought. Nested thinking.

Synthesizing is thinking at its best. How interesting to note that the term *synthesis* is used in virtually every discipline, including biology, technology, physics, music, and business! To be successful at any complex task requires the ability to synthesize. The explicit teaching of this thinking strategy prepares our students for their futures, wherever they might be.

Teaching synthesizing can be tough, however. It is sometimes hard for students to grasp and sometimes difficult for us to teach. I see concrete launching lessons as critical here. A concrete approach steadily supports our students as we release responsibility while helping us understand the complexities for ourselves. Synthesizing is all about fusing our learning, unlearning, and relearning. It's about valuing the process of our thinking, becoming reflective thinkers, remembering where we came from and where we're going. It's about *keeping the change*.

Launching Sequence: Synthesizing
Concrete Experience: Nesting Dolls

Materials needed: one set of nesting dolls, also called matryoshka (If you need a set, try searching the Oriental Trading Company's catalog, visiting one of the many Internet stores devoted to nesting dolls, or stopping by an antique mall.)

My love of nesting dolls has continued into adulthood. One of my most treasured possessions is a mahogany bookcase that holds dozens of sets of nesting dolls from all over the world. If you're going to have an obsession, I reason, nesting dolls is a good one to have. They are inexpensive to collect and not too difficult to find. I use a set of nesting dolls to launch the strategy of synthesizing, taking advantage of the fact that kids love nesting dolls, too.

I begin by pulling kids in close, around a low table or desk. On the table I place a nesting doll set, with the individual dolls lined up in ascending order. (See Figure 8–1.)

Sometimes I start with a question: "How could these nesting dolls represent your thinking?" It is typically later in the school year when I teach synthe-

Figure 8–1 *A set of nesting dolls, or matryoshka*

sizing lessons in classrooms, and by this time the students have had practice in turning my concrete objects into models of thinking. Here are some responses I've overheard when I asked kids to turn and talk:

- The bigger I get, the bigger my thinking gets!

- I grow and change and so does my thinking.

- It reminds me of what happens in cartoons when a snowball rolls down a hill.

- When I read new information I just add it on to the stuff I already know.

- My thinking used to be one thing, but now it is something else.

After the kids have sufficient time to explore their thinking, I ask them to watch me as I silently put the nesting dolls together, starting with the smallest one. The largest doll stands alone, with the smaller dolls nestled inside. Again, I ask the students to compare this model to their thinking.

- Big ideas are made up of little ideas.

- You can't always tell how much thinking happened to get to a big idea.

- We hold all of our thinking inside of us.

- Our best thinking starts out with something small.

During our study of synthesizing, I leave the nesting dolls displayed in plain view as a reminder of our changing thinking.

Note: A great picture book to use along with this launching lesson is *The Littlest Matryoshka,* by Corinne Demas Bliss (1999).

Sensory Exercises: Synthesizing

Spiraling Out of Control!

A good visual model to use to represent synthesizing is the spiral. Original thinking is central, with new thoughts and information adding new rings as you read. Kids can relate to this design: spiral slides at the playground, spiral notebooks, spiral lollipops, cinnamon rolls. The spiral lends itself to the tracking of our evolving thinking. As I watched some fifth-grade girls writing "spiral notes" to each other during indoor recess, I wondered what took me so long to think of the spiral as a response option!

I always model the use of the spiral organizer with my thinking first, using short text like a song or a poem. I read the title aloud and show the cover or illustrations. In the center of a piece of chart paper, I write down my initial response to the piece, curling my words around into a small spiral. As I continue to read or listen to the words, I add new thinking. I refer to the chart of thinking stems for synthesizing to help me craft my responses. (See Figure 8–2.)

Before their eyes, the spiral gets larger as my thinking grows and changes. The spiral pictured in Figure 8–3 reveals my changing thinking about the poem "Snow Day" by Billy Collins (2001).

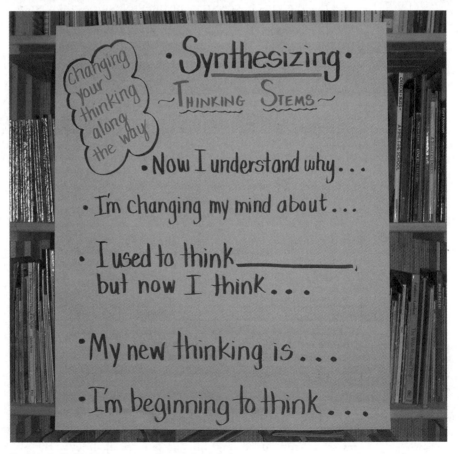

Figure 8–2 *Thinking stems for synthesizing*

Teaching Tip: Don't affix the chart paper on an easel or chalkboard. You'll need to be able to turn the paper as you write.

After the students see me model this synthesis of my thinking, they can't wait to try it out in their own notebooks...and start spiraling out of control!

Go on a Synthesizing Spree

There are countless other ways to demonstrate synthesizing to students in your classroom. Here are a few to try!

- Bring to class a box of Wonka Everlasting Gobstoppers (made by Nestle), a candy that is available at most major drugstore chains. The picture on the box shows how this treat is constructed: layer upon

Figure 8–3 *My spiral thinking about Billy Collins' "Snow Day"*

layer of colorful candy shell. Facilitate a conversation about synthe-sizing while students enjoy a Gobstopper of their own. The layers of "thinking" disappear one by one, revealing the original "thought" at the center. This candy is a perfect model of unpacking your thinking!

▩ Use a purple onion as a concrete model of synthesizing. Demonstrate how the layers of this bulb symbolize how your thinking grows as you read, either by peeling back the layers one at a time or by slicing the onion to show a cross section (slice the onion under water if you are highly sensitive).

▩ Do you know a musician or music teacher who has a synthesizer (elec-tronic keyboard)? These instruments take simple electronic sounds and combine them to make more complex variations. A synthesizer demonstration can be very interesting to students, and it can parallel the thinking process of synthesizing while reading.

▩ Post clichés about growth and change around the room. What do your students think they mean? How do they relate to your thinking?

Change your mind

Great oaks from little acorns grow

Change is good

Grow like a weed

Change your ways

▩ Label tangram pieces with the names of the comprehension strate-gies, showing how all of the strategies are independent of each other, yet part of the whole structure of thinking (thanks to third-grade teacher Debbie Funk for creating this great idea). (See Figure 8–4.)

Sing a Song of Synthesis

Many childhood songs and rhymes are structured on a spiral, where each new verse builds upon the previous one. These are ideal for showing how thinking can grow without losing the original thought that started it all. Although many kids are familiar with these songs and rhymes, it is increas-ingly common for kids to be unacquainted with them. Try these out with

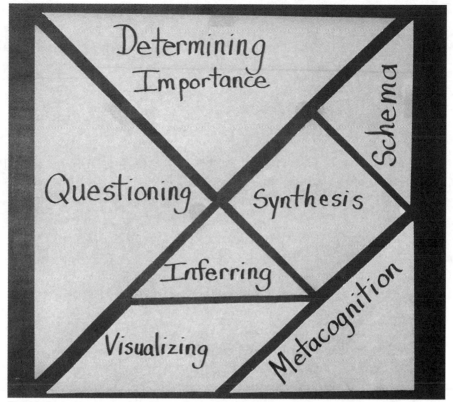

Figure 8–4 *Music teacher Margo Johnson uses this synthesizing tangram with her K–5 students*

your students, paying special attention to the structure of the lyrics and/or the melody. Ask them to identify how these songs follow the same path as their thinking when they are synthesizing!

- "There Was an Old Lady Who Swallowed a Fly" (song and rhyme)

- "The Green Grass Grows All Around" (song)

- "The House That Jack Built" (rhyme)

A popular song that models synthesis both lyrically and musically is "Windmills of Your Mind," written by Alan Bergman and Michel LeGrand, best known as the theme from the movie *The Thomas Crown Affair*. The lyrics compare thinking to many concrete models that kids can relate to: circles and spirals, snowballs rolling down a mountain, ripples in the water from a pebble. "Windmills of Your Mind" has been recorded by many artists, including Noel Harrison, Dusty Springfield, and Sting. While your students listen to the lyrics, have them sketch or make notes about the different images they hear that represent what synthesizing is like.

I. M. Pei: Structures of Synthesis

Ieoh Ming Pei is one of the most successful architects of the twentieth century. Since the mid-1950s, I. M. Pei has been the imaginative force behind some of the world's most interesting architectural structures, such as the pyramids of the Louvre in Paris, France (1989), and the Rock and Roll Hall of Fame in Cleveland, Ohio (1995). Pei, a Chinese American, was born in 1917. He founded his own architectural firm in 1955, working there until his retirement in 1990.

Pei is a master of synthesis. His abstract forms merge stone, concrete, glass, and steel into structures that redefine modernist architecture. Pei even sees the architectural process as a kind of synthesis: "The practice of architecture is a collective enterprise, with many individuals of various disciplines and talents working closely together. And from the commissioning to the completion of a project, there are also the many individuals for whom architects work, whose contribution to quality is frequently as crucial as that of the architect" (1983 Pritzker Prize Acceptance Speech).

Photographs of Pei's creations abound on the Internet and in public libraries. Present images of these structures to your students, allowing them to search for synthesis in materials and in form. For example, in a photograph of the Rock and Roll Hall of Fame, the combination of steel and glass is evident, but so is the merging of triangles, squares, circles, and rectangles. Pei melds all of these individual components into one spectacular creation . . . a synthesis for your eyes!

Wordless Books: Go Graphic

Graphic novels are hot. This growing genre now claims two aisles in my neighborhood bookstore! These long-form works, presented comic book style, are high interest, often with a complex story line. Although many contain mature themes, the volume of child-friendly graphic novels is increasing rapidly. Many teachers and librarians agree that graphic novels are the wonder cure for many reluctant readers, and the wordless variety is especially good for the teaching of synthesizing. New, significant information is presented in nearly every frame, with each illustration forcing the reader to assimilate new thinking. The benefits of this genre are many. Kids who read too fast are forced to slow down as they synthesize the symbols, expressions, settings, and thought bubbles of the characters. Kids who are challenged by decoding can experience deep thinking while they process each frame. Readers of all abilities can comprehend more deeply by talking through a graphic novel with a friend. One of my students, Cassidy, tells me that she can almost "feel her brain thinking" while experiencing a graphic novel.

Haven't used graphic novels? A great place to start is with the Owly series, created by Andy Runton (Top Shelf Productions). These uplifting tales, appropriate for all ages, feature a kind little owl that shows the reader what it means to be human. Themes include friendship, diversity, and the importance of hard work. Titles include *Owly: Flying Lessons*, *Owly: Just a Little Blue*, and *Owly: The Way Home and the Bittersweet Summer*. Some of Owly's adventures are published in comic book form only, great for readers with shorter stamina: *Owly: Breakin' the Ice* and *Owly: Splashing Around*. Short stories about Owly can be viewed online at www.andyrunton.com.

Quotes About Synthesizing to Get Kids Talking!

 I'm always looking to create some new synthesis and make it as fresh as possible.

—*Andy Summers, guitarist*

A mind stretched to a new idea never goes back to its original dimensions.

—*Oliver Wendell Holmes, jurist*

I try stuff. I synthesize what's of value with some of the other things I have at my disposal.

—*Herbie Hancock, keyboard player*

Love, in fact, is the agent of universal synthesis.
        —*Pierre Teilhard De Chardin, Jesuit priest*

Poetry is the synthesis of hyacinths and biscuits.
        —*Carl Sandburg, poet*

Eventually, all things merge into one, and a river runs through it.
        —*Norman Maclean, author*

The most useful piece of learning for the uses of life is to unlearn
what is untrue.
        —*Antisthenes, philosopher*

Time for Text: Synthesizing

These resources will help you put it all together! A few of these even contain more concrete ideas to try with your students.

Cunningham, Andie, and Ruth Shagoury. 2005. *Starting with Comprehension*. Portland, ME: Stenhouse. See Chapter 7, "Standing in the Waves: Synthesizing Information."

Harvey, Stephanie, and Anne Goudvis. 2000. *Strategies That Work*. Portland, ME: Stenhouse. See Chapter 10, "Synthesizing Information: The Evolution of Thought."

———. 2005. *The Comprehension Toolkit*. Portsmouth, NH: Heinemann. See Strategy Cluster Book 6, *Summarize and Synthesize*.

Miller, Debbie. 2002. *Reading with Meaning*. Portland, ME: Stenhouse. See Chapter 11, "Synthesizing Information."

Zimmerman, Susan, and Chryse Hutchins. 2003. *7 Keys to Comprehension*. New York: Three Rivers. See Chapter 6, "What's Important and Why."

Epilogue
Where the Sidewalk *Begins*

But this bridge will only take you halfway there—The last few steps
you'll have to take alone.

—*Shel Silverstein, "This Bridge"* (A Light in the Attic)

his isn't where the sidewalk ends. It is really an account of how the sidewalk begins, and how it begins *for me*. This book was never intended for those in pursuit of paint-by-number manuals and never-fail scripts. To attempt to write such a book would defy my beliefs in empowered teaching, student-guided learning, and the entitlement to creativity. My sincere hope is that the readers who spend some time with me in this book will intercept the concrete lessons, songs, and quotes and take off running down a sidewalk of their own construction.

Concrete Experience: One More for the Road

As I stepped through the doorway into Bonnie Frey's fourth-grade classroom, Mario announced, "Mrs. McGregor's here to teach us with more junk!" (My parents would be proud.) Mario's eyes glanced at my old green umbrella and then up at me. "I know what you're gonna do, Mrs. McG. You're gonna use that umbrella to teach us about thinking."

Mario was right. Using this concrete object during the last week of school was an opportunity too good to pass up. Having recently reread *Mosaic of Thought*, I was prompted by Ellin Keene and Susan Zimmermann's (1997) umbrella metaphor (pages 24 and 25) to take correction fluid and write "metacognition" across the outside of my umbrella (my friends have warned me against using this umbrella in public ever again). (See Figure E–1.)

Superstition aside, I opened my umbrella and read from *Mosaic of Thought* to these soon-to-be fifth graders, "Metacognition—thinking about one's own thinking—was an umbrella under which the other strategies fell." I asked the students to turn and talk to each other about how we could turn this umbrella into a concrete model of what we had learned this year.

Bonnie's class did not disappoint. Collectively, they decided to use sentence strips to label the umbrella. Kaleigh wrote "schema" on a white sentence strip and taped it on the underside of the umbrella, right along one of the ribs. Kaleigh's classmates called out other thinking strategies recalled from previous teaching: determining importance, questioning, inferring, visualizing, synthesizing. Kids labeled the multicolored strips and taped them on as well. (See Figure E–2.)

Figure E–1 *Jamie holds the metacognition umbrella*

Figure E–2 *Anthony reveals the strategy labels we created*

"What are you thinking now? Does this make sense to you? How does this concrete model help you reflect on your learning from the year?" As I circulated through the group, I noticed the students making eye contact, having relaxed conversations in groups of two and three, and staying on topic for a long period of time. I overheard kids using the language of strategic thinking, centering their talk around the concrete model, and reflecting upon things we'd talked about months before. Bonnie and I looked at each other and smiled. I guess opening an umbrella indoors isn't bad luck, after all.

Works Cited

Balliett, Blue. 2005. *Chasing Vermeer*. New York: Scholastic.

Banyai, Istvan. 1997. *REM: Rapid Eye Movement*. New York: Viking.

———. 1995a. *Re-Zoom*. New York: Viking.

———. 1995b. *Zoom*. New York: Viking.

———. 2005. *The Other Side*. San Francisco: Chronicle.

Bliss, Corinne Demas. 1999. *The Littlest Matryoshka*. New York: Hyperion Books for Children.

Carmi, Giora. 2003. *A Circle of Friends*. New York: Star Bright.

Carson, Rachel. 1998. *The Sense of Wonder*. New York: HarperCollins.

Chevalier, Tracy. 2001. *Girl with a Pearl Earring*. New York: Plume.

Collard, Sneed B. III. 2004. *Animals Asleep*. Boston: Houghton Mifflin.

Collins, Billy. 2001. "Snow Day." In *Sailing Alone Around the Room: New and Selected Poems*. New York: Random House.

Cunningham, Andie, and Ruth Shagoury. 2005. *Starting with Comprehension*. Portland, ME: Stenhouse.

Fleischman, Paul, and Kevin Hawkes. 2004. *Sidewalk Circus*. Cambridge, MA: Candlewick.

Gallagher, Kelly. 2004. *Deeper Reading: Comprehending Challenging Texts, 4–12*. Portland, ME: Stenhouse.

Gelb, Michael J. 1998. *How to Think Like Leonardo da Vinci: Seven Steps to Genius Every Day*. New York: Dell.

Gladwell, Malcolm. 2005. *Blink: The Power of Thinking Without Thinking*. New York: Little, Brown.

Harvey, Stephanie, and Anne Goudvis. 2005. *The Comprehension Toolkit: Language and Lessons for Active Literacy*. Portsmouth, NH: Heinemann.

———. 2000. *Strategies That Work: Teaching Comprehension to Enhance Understanding*. Portland, ME: Stenhouse.

Hoyt, Linda. 2000. *Snapshots: Literacy Minilessons Up Close*. Portsmouth, NH: Heinemann.

———. 2002. *Make It Real: Strategies for Success with Informational Texts*. Portsmouth, NH: Heinemann.

Keene, Ellin O., and Susan Zimmermann. 1997. *Mosaic of Thought: Teaching Comprehension in a Reader's Workshop*. Portsmouth, NH: Heinemann.

Lehman, Barbara. 2004. *The Red Book*. Boston: Houghton Mifflin.

L'Engle, Madeleine. 2001. *Madeleine L'Engle Herself: Reflections on a Writing Life*. Colorado Springs, CO: Shaw.

Miller, Debbie. 2002. *Reading with Meaning: Teaching Comprehension in the Primary Grades*. Portland, ME: Stenhouse.

Oczkus, Lori. 2004. *Super 6 Comprehension Strategies*. Norwood, MA: Christoper-Gordon.

Parton, Dolly. 1994. *Coat of Many Colors*. New York: HarperCollins.

Pearson, P. D., L. R. Roehler, J. A. Dole, and G. G. Duffy. 1992. "Developing Expertise in Reading Comprehension." In J. Samuels and A. Farstrup, eds., *What Research Has to Say About Reading Instruction*. Newark, DE: International Reading Association.

Pearson, P. D. and M. C. Gallagher. 1983. "The Instruction of Reading Comprehension." *Contemporary Educational Psychology* 8: 317–344.

Pei, I. M. 1983. *Pritzker Prize Acceptance Speech*, Metropolitan Museum of Art. New York.

Postman, Neil. 1995. *The End of Education: Redefining the Value of School*. New York: Vintage.

Reston, James. 2001. *Warriors of God: Richard the Lionheart and Saladin in the Third Crusade*. New York: Anchor.

Roosevelt, Franklin Delano, "On Progress of the War." Fireside Chat, Washington, D.C., February 23, 1942.

Seskin, Steve, and Allen Shamblin. 2002. *Don't Laugh at Me*. Berkeley, CA: Tricycle.

Stonehill, Randy. 1992. "Rachel Delevoryas." Nashville, TN: Stonehillian Music/Word Music.

Szymusiak, Karen, and Franki Sibberson. 2001. *Beyond Leveled Books*. Portland, ME: Stenhouse.

Tovani, Cris. 2000. *I Read It, but I Don't Get It: Comprehension Strategies for Adolescent Readers*. Portland, ME: Stenhouse.

Vreeland, Susan. 2000. *Girl in Hyacinth Blue*. New York: Penguin.

Wiesner, David. 1988. *Free Fall*. New York: Lothrop, Lee, and Shepard.

———. 1991. *Tuesday*. New York: Clarion.

———. 1999. *Sector 7*. New York: Clarion.

Wilhelm, Jeffrey. 2004. *Reading IS Seeing: Learning to Visualize Scenes, Characters, Ideas, and Text Worlds to Improve Comprehension and Reflective Reading*. New York: Scholastic.

Zimmermann, Susan, and Chryse Hutchins. 2003. *7 Keys to Comprehension: How to Help Your Kids Read It and Get It!* New York: Three Rivers.

Index